HOW DEEP THE MYSTERY

Meditating on the Words of the Mass

JOYCE ANN ZIMMERMAN, CPPS

LTP

LITURGY
TRAINING
PUBLICATIONS

Nihil Obstat
Rev. Mr. Daniel G. Welter, JD
Chancellor
Archdiocese of Chicago
July 30, 2019

Imprimatur
Most Rev. Ronald A. Hicks
Vicar General
Archdiocese of Chicago
July 30, 2019

The *Nihil Obstat* and *Imprimatur* are declarations that the material is free from doctrinal or moral error, and thus is granted permission to publish in accordance with c. 827. No legal responsibility is assumed by the grant of this permission. No implication is contained herein that those who have granted the *Nihil Obstat* and *Imprimatur* agree with the content, opinions, or statements expressed.

Timothy A. Johnston edited this book. Christian Rocha was the production editor, and Juan Alberto Castillo was the designer and production artist.

Cover art: *Living Water* by Linda McCray © lindamccray.com. Used with permission.

Chapter art by Nina Warner.

24 23 22 21 20   1 2 3 4 5

Printed in Canada

Library of Congress Control Number: 2019950070

ISBN 978-1-61671-515-1

HDM

CONTENTS

INTRODUCTION

It's a different world in which we live! Any forty-something person and younger does not remember a time without computers, cell phones, and a ton of other electronic gadgets that make communication instant and easy. Technology in all forms has crowded into our lives. Recently I went to a wedding website where a couple had posted in neat categories everything to do with their upcoming big day. Out of curiosity, I clicked on the gift registry tab. Gone were requests for toasters and linens and dishes! In their place were requests for electronic gadgets of every kind and price. Yes, it's a very different world!

Commentaries abound on the pros and cons of all this technology. True, it makes our lives much easier. Quite frankly, I love GPS; it's like having a copilot in the car with me and frees me to keep my eyes on the road and traffic while a voice prompts me for turns to get me to my destination safely. My cell phone enables me to call the person meeting me at an airport, informing him or her that I've arrived. At the same time, we've all seen the TV commercials (and even on occasion observed in real time) people sitting across from each other texting messages rather than actually speaking to each other. Psychologists and educators have noted that we are losing the art of writing, reading, of communicating. And with this loss, comes a greater loss: we are all too often not connected with each other except through gadgets.

There is increasing talk in liturgical circles about how all this technology impacts liturgy. The questions go way beyond how appropriate it is to have large projection screens in the sacred space; for example, can digital projections replace holding a hymnal? Or can the convenience of an iPad replace a liturgical book? The answers to these and many other questions that continue to arise are not so simple. What are the liturgical principles that must guide us in dealing with liturgy and technology? This is a question that *Sacrosanctum Concilium* (*The Constitution on the Sacred Liturgy* from the Second Vatican Council) does not directly address. Most of the technology we've grown to love and depend on didn't even exist when this foundational Vatican II document was approved on December 4, 1963.

Getting at the Heart of Liturgy

No matter where technology takes us, and no matter how we use it to make our preparation and celebration of liturgy better, the most basic principle about liturgy never changes. Liturgy is a celebration of the Paschal Mystery.[1] As such, liturgy always deals with a mystery—the Mystery of Christ and the salvation he came to bring us. Because liturgy enacts a mystery, we can never understand it fully, we can never contain it, we can never exhaust its meaning. Over the centuries since the Last Supper, the rituals surrounding our response to Jesus' command to "Do this in remembrance of me"[2] have changed greatly; for example, the earliest strata of the Eucharistic celebration took place within a shared meal.[3] Then its present fourfold structure developed, consisting of introduction, Liturgy of the Word, Liturgy of the Eucharist, and dismissal. During the resurgence of the Holy Roman Empire, various court practices crept in when civil and ecclesial societies pretty much collapsed into one. Abuses happened, and abuses were corrected. No matter where we are on the historical spectrum of Eucharistic celebrations, the one issue of obedience to Jesus' command remains.

It is possible for liturgical celebration to become simply rubric-oriented in order to "get it right." But clearly this approach is not consistent with a holy response to Jesus' command. While we are always careful to celebrate liturgy the way the Church prescribes and with great reverence and dignity, far more important than "getting it right" is praying it well. Liturgy invites us into Christ's Mystery, into the total self-giving that the Paschal Mystery is truly about. Over the entire history of liturgy, we have been searching and trying ritual ways that draw us deeper into the Mystery being celebrated. And, again, we will never exhaust the richness of that mystery.

The implementation of the third edition of *The Roman Missal* took place on the First Sunday of Advent, 2011. This new translation caused consternation for some people, and still does for a few, but most are used to it by now. While many people acknowledge that this is not a perfect translation (nor will one ever be perfect!), it is helpful to understand it within the context of the whole development of the structure and meaning of liturgy. The translation is one more step toward what the Church at this time feels is necessary and helpful for responding better to Jesus' command. One of the most distinctive features of the new translation is that it more closely adheres to the Latin *editio typica* (official edition) and, therefore, includes many rich images and phrases not translated in previous US English editions. These images and phrases not only help draw us into an appropriate sacred prayer language during liturgical celebrations, but they also can be rich springboards for our own personal prayer. Praying these texts privately opens us to hear them anew when praying them communally during liturgical celebrations.

---

1. See *Sacrosanctum Concilium*, 6 and 106.
2. Luke 22:19.
3. See 1 Corinthians 11:17–34.

Anything worth doing is worth taking time to prepare well. The more important the task, the more time and care we spend in preparation. Surely this truism applies to our celebration of liturgy! Many faithful Catholics have developed the habit of reading and praying the Scriptures and Mass texts for any given Sunday before they ever leave for church. This laudable practice fixes these texts and prayers in our "ears," so to speak, and so when we hear them we are much more apt to let the words sink more deeply into our hearts, readying us to encounter Christ in his Mystery ever more profoundly. Possibly less fixed in our ears are the texts of the "ordinary" of the Mass itself—not so much the changeable texts, but the texts we hear time and time again. Here the challenge is to tune in familiar words, not letting them slip by us because we know them so well. The 2011 translation affords us an opportunity to hear familiar texts in a new way. One way to help ourselves pray these and the proper (changeable) texts better during Mass is to use them for our personal prayer.

How This Book Unfolds

Many books have been published about *The Roman Missal,* third edition, but they are generally about this sacred liturgical text. This book is different. It is a book helping readers to pray the liturgical texts themselves outside an actual liturgical celebration. So, in a real sense *How Deep the Mystery: Meditating on the Words of the Mass* is a personal prayer book.

This book is divided into five parts, drawing from the different kinds of text in the Eucharistic liturgy with which we are most familiar: Ordinary of the Mass, Collects, Prefaces, Eucharistic Prayers, and Blessings and Dismissals. Each part includes fifteen different prayer experiences. Obviously, the seventy-five texts will be those that strike me and surely do not exhaust all the rich prayer possibilities the texts of the Eucharistic liturgy offer. I chose texts according to what the people hear and pray most often while at Mass. But by no means are these the only texts in *The Roman Missal* that readily lead to prayer. Once the reader has prayed this book, he or she is encouraged to go to other texts and continue praying with many more of the sacred texts of *The Roman Missal* (easily available in the many daily and Sunday missals being published). In this way, this book is not one that is simply read or prayed once and then set aside; it is a resource that the reader can come back to again and again as well as a method by which the reader can choose other texts from *The Roman Missal* to pray.

In these prayer experiences, I am inviting the reader into my own personal practice of using Mass texts for personal prayer (as much as is possible through a printed medium). For each experience, the liturgical text is printed out for the convenience of the reader; we might read a passage more than once, and reading out loud sometimes is very helpful so we can listen to the words through the sound of our own voice. If a particular word or phrase pops out and begs to be savored, then do that; the quantity of words we read is not important.

I include a brief reflection with each passage, which helps us open ourselves to prayer and an encounter with God not only during this private prayer time, but also during the celebration of liturgy itself. Hopefully, the reader is also drawn to supply his or her own words and images; don't be hampered by my reflections! These reflections are given as a guide, not as a final product. The reflections printed in this book are simply to get the prayer process started, and the reader continues the process by spending time responding to the open-ended statements at the end of each reflection. Finally, I conclude each reflection with a prayer; again, the reader is also encouraged to add to this printed prayer or even simply use his or her own words for this prayer.

Origin of This Book

Like so many other liturgical educators, prior to the implementation of *The Roman Missal*, third edition, in 2011 I was crisscrossing the country facilitating workshops on the new translation and its implementation. I was forcefully struck by participants' responses each time I shared with participants the richness of some of the phrases and images the new translation includes. Many people began to offer their own insights. One evening after a particularly stimulating day, it dawned on me that perhaps a new kind of book on *The Roman Missal* would be well received.

Over the last few years, there have been many publications on *The Roman Missal*, third edition. Some have been scholarly, some pastoral. Most have addressed issues about *The Roman Missal*—its translation, syntax, structure, implementation, pastoral acceptance, etc. A few books have been published that have addressed how to pray *The Roman Missal*, but to my knowledge no book has been published to date that uses actual texts from *The Roman Missal* to stimulate personal prayer. This book does just that. It is a guide for people to pray with the texts of *The Roman Missal* so that during the actual celebration of Mass and other liturgies they are more attuned to the style of liturgical language and how it can draw us more deeply into prayer, into the Mystery we celebrate.

Because this book originated from the enthusiasm and insights of ordinary folks in the pews, this book is intended to be pastoral in scope, appealing to anyone—clergy, liturgical ministers, assembly members—who celebrates with *The Roman Missal*. It is intended as a prayer book, drawing people into the rich reflective and prayer possibilities of the new translation. May our prayer—liturgical and personal—be rich in insight, full with meaning, fraught with mystery, and lead to communion with the God who gives the Divine Self to us in such lavish ways.

CHAPTER 1

TEXTS DRAWN FROM THE ORDINARY OF THE MASS

The Ordinary of the Mass is not really very "ordinary," except in the sense that it is the text from Mass that is prayed at every single Mass. The Ordinary of the Mass does not change with the season or feast day. *The Roman Missal* does, however, include some choices for a few of the ordinary texts so we don't always hear or speak the same words. For example, there are several choices for how the priest greets us at the beginning of Mass, a choice of whether there is a Penitential Act or Blessing and Sprinkling of Water, and a choice of whether to profess the Nicene or Apostles' Creed.

Because these texts are so familiar to us, they may seem to be unimportant. Yet they are the backbone of the Mass. They are the known structure which holds all the other changeable (called "Propers") elements of the Mass together into a unified whole. We begin by praying some of these familiar texts. Through our prayer and reflection, may we come to appreciate more keenly God's calling us into Divine Presence.

1.1   COMMUNION OF THE HOLY SPIRIT

Roman Missal Text

> The grace of our Lord Jesus Christ,
> and the love of God,
> and the communion of the Holy Spirit
> be with you all.
>
> —no. 2[1]

Reflection

The priest, who is the visible presence of Christ, the Head of his Body, the Church, greets us at the beginning of the Eucharistic celebration. The beautiful words of this greeting are found at the very end of St. Paul's Second Letter to the Corinthians (2 Corinthians 13:13)—words of Sacred Scripture, words that are a sacred text. This is not just any greeting; it is a greeting that acknowledges our great dignity as a gathered assembly. We are the Body of Christ, the Church made visible in this very gathering for liturgy.

This is a short text, but one which points us to God's Trinitarian presence. Just before we are thus greeted, we together make the Sign of the Cross. Now we are greeted with how the Divine Persons of the Holy Trinity desire to be one with us. Our celebration of Mass is an encounter with the three Persons of the Holy Trinity, one God who chooses to be present to us.

The grace of our Lord Jesus Christ . . . What is this "grace" we are given? We often think of grace as a quantity to be had: we get grace for doing this or that. We get grace when we celebrate the Eucharist. We get grace when we do a kind deed for another. We get grace for faithfully living the Gospel. While all this is true, what exactly do we "get"? Actually, grace is not some "thing," but is the very Life of God. Being given this Life means that we are in a most intimate relationship with each Person of the Trinity. Further, sharing in Christ's risen Life through Baptism means that we are one with him in a unique way. This is who we are: the Body of Christ. We share his identity. We are his Presence now.

the love of God . . . Love is a much-used word these days, and most of its uses are best forgotten. It is so wonderful to be greeted at the beginning of Mass with a love that is Life-giving, with a love that is ever faithful, with a love that is forever creating us into more perfect images of God. The love of God goes beyond any love of our imagining. It is a love that brings us into being, sustains our life, nourishes our hearts, welcomes our weaknesses, and embraces us into the fullness

---

1. *The Roman Missal* numbers paragraphs in order to refer to its texts more easily. In order to keep notes to a minimum during our prayers, we will simply include the reference numbers to *The Roman Missal* after the text. Unless otherwise indicated, reference numbers are to the Order of Mass within *The Roman Missal*.

of Life. It is a love that draws us into intimacy with our Triune Creator, an intimacy that is fulfilling and fruitful. It is a love that reminds us about what love really is, self-giving made visible.

the communion of the Holy Spirit . . . Just one word in Latin, *communio*, requires a whole gamut of English words to capture the depth of its meaning: unity, participation with, one with, together, strengthening. Our communion with the Holy Spirit is far more than some kind of pleasant connection with a Divine Being. It is a choice by God to be completely empathetic with our human lot, to be involved with our affairs, to be the Divine Source of our strength. God is not "out there," apart from us. God is one with us, supporting and encouraging us in all we are and do. Further, this communion is nourished and strengthened by Word and Sacrament, and in this greeting, we are encouraged to surrender ourselves to the divine intimacy to which we are called. The Holy Spirit dwells within each of us and makes this communion with the divine possible.

There is a movement in this greeting from graced relationship to divine love to unity. Indeed, this movement describes God's great desire to care for us in ways we cannot even imagine. We are greeted—and reminded—that our relationship with God is initiated by God, given an intimate shape by God, and draws us into being one with God. Such a greeting! Such a relationship! Such a wondrous mystery!

To Ponder

- What I need to do at the beginning of Mass in order for the Sign of the Cross and this Trinitarian greeting to make a difference in how I surrender to God's presence and call is . . .

- God's grace and love and oneness with me urges me to . . .

Prayer

Wondrous and triune God,
you love us into existence,
sustain us by your grace,
and remain one with us in both our weakness and strength.
Open us to your ever-abiding Divine Presence,
draw us to your divine love,
and help us love others with your care and compassion.
We ask this in the name of Jesus Christ our Lord,
in the unity of the Holy Spirit,
one God for ever and ever. Amen.

1.2   I Have Greatly Sinned

Roman Missal Text

> I confess to almighty God
> and to you, my brothers and sisters,
> that I have greatly sinned . . .
>
> —no. 4

Reflection

There is much talk about sin these days. Some lament that we have lost our sense of sin. Some think our entire world is evil and sin lurks around every corner ready to bite us even when we are least expecting. We all know that sin is a deliberate act. It cannot sneak up on us. We also know that as human beings we inherit a tendency to put others and ourselves before God; we tend to weaken the very relationships that give us Life, and to omit doing whatever conforms us closer to Christ. We also tend to think of sin in terms of discrete acts of omission or commission rather than an attitude, habit, or way of being that becomes a stumbling block on our journey into Christ and the Life he offers us.

The Penitential Act at the beginning of Mass is not the Sacrament of Penance. Our confession of sinfulness here has an entirely different (though certainly not unrelated) purpose. In the sacrament we commonly call "confession," we examine our conscience on how well we have lived the Gospel, express our sorrow for wrongdoing, and seek conversion of life that brings us closer to Christ and one another. In the Penitential Act that (usually) begins Mass, the focus is less on individual confession of sin and conversion (which is the focus of the Sacrament of Penance) as it is on emptying ourselves of hindrances that keep us from opening our hearts to God so that we might celebrate Mass worthily. Gently, we want to rid ourselves of whatever keeps us from surrendering to God's mercy and love, grace and transformation, peace and forgiveness. This opening of ourselves to God's merciful Presence creates the inner space for God to enter into our lives in ever new and surprising ways.

I have greatly sinned . . . Really? Our words might lead us to think that we and our gathered brothers and sisters live our lives far from God. Our very presence at Mass witnesses that God is not far from us, that we want to live good lives, that we do not want to stray from the path of justice and truth. Are we really *great* sinners? For the most part, we are not. So how can we pray these words with deep meaning?

It is fascinating that people whom we consider very holy often declare themselves to be great sinners. This is a common thread in the writings of great mystics like St. Teresa of Avila. St. Teresa of Calcutta, in our own time, often spoke about her great sense of being a sinner and unworthy of God's great gifts and love. How can such holy people think themselves great sinners?

When we think of sin in terms of relationships, we might gain an insight into what we are truly confessing in the Confiteor. When we love someone deeply, even minor transgressions that cause him or her hurt or anguish bother us greatly. The more we love someone, the less we want to do anything that weakens the relationship, the less we want to do anything that keeps us from falling more deeply in love with the other and deepening the bond of that unique relationship. The same is true with our relationship with God.

When we are "young" in the spiritual life, we might do things and have attitudes or habits that disrupt relationships with God and others. But as we grow in our love for God, we work at the kind of conversion of life that helps us grow in our relationships. But a curious thing happens on this spiritual journey. We overcome one kind of sinful behavior only to become aware of another. And the more we fall in love with God—the more real this love becomes in our lives—the more do small things that we hardly gave two thoughts to earlier in our spiritual journey now loom up to be great barriers to deepening a relationship. Now even little things seem great because we want to avoid anything at all that gets in the way of simply basking in God's great love for us and returning our love to God.

Here is the paradox: the more we grow in loving relationship, the more the little hurts loom as greater hurts. So our confession of "I have greatly sinned" can actually be a profound profession of our growth in love for God and others. We have grown spiritually in a way that we want nothing at all to stand between God and us. Becoming more keenly aware of how we have greatly sinned can actually be interpreted as a profession of holiness.

To Ponder

- I am most aware of sinfulness in my life when . . .

- I am most aware of God's grace in my life when . . .

- I witness to my own growth in holiness in these ways . . .

Prayer

Holy and loving God,
you shower upon us the most abundant blessings
as you call us to your Divine Presence,
instill in us your very Life,
and gift us with your Son and Spirit,
who help us to live the Gospel well.
Be with us as we strive to live holy lives,
and help us to avoid any action, habit, or attitude
that mars the wonderful and grace-filled relationship
with you and each other
to which you have invited us.
We ask this through Christ our Lord. Amen.

1.3   LORD, HAVE MERCY

Roman Missal Text

Lord, have mercy. Lord, have mercy.
Christ, have mercy. Christ, have mercy.
Lord, have mercy. Lord, have mercy.

—no. 7

Reflection

When the Confiteor is used in the Penitential Act, it is followed by this triple invocation to Jesus Christ. Many of us know this element by its Greek text, *Kyrie, eléison; Christe, eléison.* This is the only Greek text in the Roman liturgy, and it is very ancient in origin. Sometimes this invocation was prayed in a litany form, similar to how it is used presently in the Litany of Saints, where the Kyrie begins the litany. Sometimes it was used in the context of what is now our Universal Prayer (Prayer of the Faithful), where the "Lord, have mercy" was the people's response to the intercessions. Nor was it only used at Mass. It was included in some forms of the early Liturgy of the Hours. All of this suggests to us that our reliance on God's mercy for our well-being has been an important part of our Christian tradition.

The "Lord, have mercy" is a fitting text following the Confiteor, where it is found in our present Eucharistic liturgy. We are encouraged by and honest in confessing our sinfulness to God because he is merciful, forgiving, and compassionate. The entire history of God's relationship to God's beloved people has been one where God constantly turns away from harsh retribution when we have erred; God only asks that we repent and then acts most graciously toward us. One only needs to pray the Psalms to have a great sense of God's generous mercy. Over and over again the Psalms remind us of God's graciousness and healing. Over and over again the Psalms remind us that God never forsakes us.

We are confident in God's mercy because God has never failed to forgive and show great compassion toward us if we but ask. The repetition of this brief invocation serves to underscore the importance of that for which we are asking: the Lord's mercy. It does not do for us to ask for God's mercy only once; we do so again and again, recognizing that our weak human nature tends to waver on our journey toward salvation. The repetition also serves to embolden us in our asking for God's forgiveness and mercy.

We might think of the "Lord, have mercy" from another perspective, too. If God forgives us so freely and generously, then ought we not forgive others and have mercy on those who wrong or hurt us? It is a contradiction to rejoice in God's mercy and then show no mercy toward others. It is a shameful thing to receive God's forgiveness if we ourselves fail to forgive others. The Our Father reminds us of this. Perhaps this is why we pray the Our Father each time we celebrate Mass. They are demanding words: we ask God to forgive us as we forgive others. If we are not forgiving and merciful to others, then we mock God's free gift to us.

What a good thing, in our preparing ourselves to celebrate Mass well, that we acknowledge our sinfulness and seek God's mercy! What a good thing to be constantly reminded of how forgiving God is to us! What a good thing to know that God wishes us to surrender ourselves into the Divine Presence, open ourselves to God's gracious mercy, and deepen our relationship with God and each other! We say again and again: Lord, have mercy. More than simply petition, these words instill in us the confidence that we are right with God. They can serve as a bridge between the acknowledgment of our sinfulness and what follows (on Sundays and high feast days) as our great hymn of praise, the Glory to God. Experiencing God's mercy, we cannot help but lift our hearts in praise.

To Ponder

- Times when I am most acutely aware of my need for God's mercy are . . .

- I experience that mercy in the depth of my heart when . . .

- I am led to show mercy toward others when . . .

Prayer

Loving-kind, merciful God,
you know well our weakness
as well as our heart's desire to be in right relationship with you.
Show us your mercy
that we might show others that same mercy.
Forgive us that we might forgive others.
Help us to be faithful to you and the way of the Gospel
that we might witness to others your great compassion and care.
We ask this through Christ our Lord. Amen.

1.4 WE GIVE YOU THANKS FOR YOUR GREAT GLORY

Roman Missal Text

Glory to God in the highest,
and on earth peace to people of good will.
We praise you,
we bless you,
we adore you,
we glorify you,
we give you thanks for your great glory,
Lord God, heavenly King,
O God, almighty Father.
Lord Jesus Christ, Only Begotten Son,
Lord God, Lamb of God, Son of the Father,
you take away the sins of the world,
    have mercy on us;
you take away the sins of the world,
    receive our prayer;
you are seated at the right hand of the Father,
    have mercy on us.

For you alone are the Holy One,
you alone are the Lord,
you alone are the Most High,
Jesus Christ,
with the Holy Spirit,
in the glory of God the Father.
Amen.

—no. 8

Reflection

Glory to God . . . We notice that this great song of praise opens with a sentence without a verb, but with strong acclamations. Echoing the song of the angels on the night of Jesus' birth in Bethlehem, with them we acclaim—no, we shout—God's greatness and God's wondrous deeds on our behalf. Having acknowledged our sinfulness and begged and received God's mercy, our hearts can't help but spill over in a great song of praise. The opening two lines of the Glory to God deserve an exclamation point at the end of each line! It does not do to sing them quietly. They require full voice, full throat, and full heart.

Our hearts continue to overflow during a litany. With short, can't-be-missed, tumbling-over-each-other-in-eagerness sentences, we praise, bless, adore, and glorify God. It is as though we need four different verbs to try to capture what our hearts are trying to express. In the end, we simply give God thanks for God's "great glory." Our God has dealt with us human beings in wondrous ways. We have just experienced in this first part of the Eucharistic liturgy God's forgiveness and mercy. We also sing about this as we acclaim Jesus as the one who "take[s] away the sins of the world." For this, we glorify God. Soon we will experience Jesus' continual self-giving to us in the Holy Communion of his very Body and Blood. For this, we glorify Jesus Christ. All of these actions are "with the Holy Spirit," whose wisdom and joy dwelling within us enable us to sing this great hymn of praise.

God's glory is nothing less than the traces of the Divine Trinity in our midst. God's glory is the manifestation of God's Presence. At numerous times during Mass we pause to remember God's mighty deeds on our behalf: in the Scriptures proclaimed, in the Profession of Faith, and in the Eucharistic Prayer. These are weighty deeds; God never acts frivolously towards us. God's actions on our behalf always have consequences for our well-being. When we experience God's presence in so many ways—forgiveness, mercy, grace, life, and Life (God's very essence), healing, creation, beauty, sustenance—we are in the presence of God's glory. These traces of God's loving deeds on our behalf invite us to become ever more aware of God's love and care, of God's abiding Presence, of God's touching our humanity with the grace of divinity.

We conclude this hymn celebrating the Incarnation and God's Presence with a Trinitarian nod: Jesus Christ, . . . Holy Spirit, . . . God the Father. God's glory—the visible traces of God's Presence and deeds—is always a Trinitarian glory. Our hymn recognizes the great mystery of Three-in-One. While we sing of God's great deeds on our behalf by remembering the Incarnation and salvation of the Lamb of God, we also sing of God's one Divine Being within the unity of the Three Persons. Our doxology—our praising, our blessing, our adoring, our giving God glory—is always Trinitarian and, as such, always integrates all the divine actions of the Three Persons on our behalf, even when we don't specifically mention them. Our giving God glory can never be limited by our experiences but always opens us to the immensity and mystery of God.

To Ponder

- For the Glory to God to become a great and full-voiced hymn of praise for me, I must . . .

- The Glory to God speaks to me of . . . I experience God's presence to me in all these ways . . .

- My heart bursts with praise when . . .

Prayer

Glorious God of creation and salvation,
you make known to us your mighty deeds
through the events and experiences of our own lives.
May we always be attentive to your glory,
    that trace of your Divine Presence made visible to us.
May we respond to your presence with joy and fidelity
as we strive to be ever more faithful to your holy will.
May we continually thank and praise you for your gifts to us.
We ask this through Christ our Lord. Amen.

1.5   Desire for the Lord's Presence

Roman Missal Text

> The Lord be with you.
> And with your spirit.
>
> —no. 15 and elsewhere

Reflection

This wish-greeting is exchanged rarely during Mass, only occurring three, sometimes four times: optionally at the beginning of the Introductory Rites (no. 2); always at the beginning of the Gospel proclamation (no. 15), at the beginning of the Eucharistic Prayer as the first of the Preface dialogues (no. 31), and at the beginning of the Concluding Rites (no. 141). Notice, this wish-greeting marks the beginning of three major divisions of the Eucharistic liturgy: Introductory Rites, Liturgy of the Eucharist (the presentation and preparation of the gifts are preparatory rites for this part of the Mass), and Concluding Rites. We also notice that rather than beginning the Liturgy of the Word (as in the other three cases), it is deferred to the beginning of the proclamation of the Gospel. This shift in placement points to the centrality of the Gospel proclamation in the Liturgy of the Word. This rich greeting and response alerts us to the Gospel proclamation as something quite different from the other readings.

Sometimes a priest or deacon changes this wish to a factual statement: The Lord *is* with you. This is the form of salutation Gabriel used in addressing Mary at the Annunciation (see Luke 1:28). However, it is a different grammatical form from what we usually find in Sacred Scripture (see, for example, Ruth 2:4). "The Lord be with you" is an expressed wish or desire that has more import than a simple statement of fact. In early Christian assemblies, it preceded the invitation to pray, giving both hope and credence to Jesus' promise that "where two or three are gathered in my name, I am there among them" (Matthew 18:20). We are confident that our prayer is heard because the One to whom we raise our prayer is present to us and with us and in us.

The response to this wish-greeting, in the translation of *The Roman Missal*, third edition, captures the original Latin, *Et cum spiritu tuo*, and is much richer in meaning than the simple, former translation of "And also with you." The Scriptural understanding of the human person recognized one's "spirit" as the whole being in its fullness. So, for example, when Mary in her response to Elizabeth acclaims "my spirit rejoices in God my Savior" (Luke 1:47), it is an enthusiastic utterance—her whole being quivers with the joy of what God is and will accomplish in and through her. We can well imagine that Mary was dancing on her tippy-toes as her heart overflowed in praise.

Our own response to being greeted with "The Lord be with you" must be as heartfelt and enthusiastic as Mary's. Our response must give witness to our eager anticipation of what might happen in the very proclamation of the Gospel. And so we are eager to wish the Lord's Presence in and to the Gospel proclaimer, be he deacon or priest. We are anticipating his proclamation to be lively with Divine Presence, welling up from the fullness of his being, and rich with encouragement for our hearing the Gospel not as mere words but as a way of life. This wish-greeting and our response enliven us and prepare us to hear the Gospel proclamation in new ways, even when we are so familiar with many of the Gospel stories. Each time we hear the Gospel proclamation we are different persons, having lived our days in the Lord's Presence. We are reminded with this greeting that we are to hear with new ears and take Jesus' words into new hearts.

To Ponder

- When I hear "The Lord be with you," I am roused to . . .
  I could make this wish-greeting more meaningful if I were to . . .

- When I respond "And with your spirit," I am roused to . . .
  I could make my response more meaningful if I were to . . .

Prayer

Almighty God,
your words to us are lively and fill us with Life.
Help us to be more aware of your abiding Presence,
to be faithful to your words and holy will,
and to respond with the fullness of our being to your goodness.
We ask this through Christ our Lord. Amen.

1.6 THE LORD IS TRULY PRESENT IN THE GOSPEL PROCLAIMED

Roman Missal Text

A reading from the holy Gospel according to N.
Glory to you, O Lord.
The Gospel of the Lord.
Praise to you, Lord Jesus Christ.

—nos. 15 and 16

Reflection

Sometimes texts are repeated so often that we simply don't hear them. This is frequently true for the Gospel parables. We have heard them year after year, we know the stories, we know how they end, and so they do not seem to carry the fascination and punch as when we hear something for the first time. This is also all too frequently true for the Mass texts themselves.

Case in point is the citation and acclamation that precede and follow the Gospel proclamation. Because these texts are so familiar, when we hear the priest's words we mostly say our response without ever thinking. These texts did not change with the recent translation of *The Roman Missal*, so we don't even have new words to shake us out of our autopilot responses. But we can examine the words we say and extract new and deeper meaning, which may help us make these words more than just responses on our lips.

The *General Instruction of The Roman Missal*[2] refers to "Glory to you, O Lord" as an acclamation (no. 134), as does the rubric of *The Roman Missal* itself (no. 15). The Latin verb *acclamare* means to cry out loudly, especially with approval and praise. But notice the words we say in direct address: *you* and *O Lord*. Because this is the Gospel (a text recording the life, words, and ministry of Jesus), we are clear that "Lord" here refers to Jesus Christ. Moreover, "you" also refers to Lord. This is direct address, words we use when we are eyeball-to-eyeball with someone, when we are speaking to someone who is actually, really present to us. Before the Gospel is even proclaimed we are shouting glory (praise, honor, adoration) to Jesus Christ, whom we address as present among us.

Similar direct address language is part of our response after the deacon or priest acclaims "The Gospel of the Lord" (no. 16) at the conclusion of the Gospel proclamation: "Praise to you, Lord Jesus Christ." Here we not only have the direct

---

2. This official document guides the celebration of the Mass. It provides instructions, both theological and functional, on the various parts and ministries of the Mass.

address pronoun *you*, but also the text makes explicit whom we address: "Lord Jesus Christ."

The structural pattern of this four-line dialogue is citation, acclamation, acclamation, response. In the very proclamation of the Gospel, Jesus Christ is present, and our words acknowledge (nay, acclaim) this. What the deacon or priest says to conclude the Gospel is no mere signal of the end of a reading; it is an announcement (nay, acclamation) of the proclamation of the Gospel as a living, dynamic Presence of the risen Christ. Our response can only be heart-filled praise of the risen Christ.

Something quite different from this happens at the beginning and end of the First and Second Readings. After the citation by the reader ("A reading from . . . ") the assembly has no response whatsoever. We simply receive information. The reader just begins the reading. At the conclusion of the reading, the reader acclaims "The word of the Lord" (no. 10) and the assembly answers "Thanks be to God." In our response, there is no direct address word.

All of this helps us point to the Gospel as unique among the readings. While all of Scripture is God's inspired Word to us, the proclaimed Gospel is even more. Liturgically, the proclamation of the Gospel has us stand in the very Presence of Jesus Christ.

Our real encounter with Christ in the very proclamation of the Gospel urges us, inspires us, commands us to identify ourselves more perfectly with the Christ in whom we have been baptized and to live as he did. Thus, the proclamation of the Gospel provides us with a blueprint for Christian living. Each Gospel proclamation reveals to us a bit more of the Mystery we are called to embrace and live. It certainly will not do for us to mumble mindlessly these two acclamation-responses to the Gospel. The urging of *The Roman Missal* to sing them would help us wake up to what we are saying, as singing takes thought and effort beyond merely saying the liturgical texts. These responses are a commitment from us to Gospel living, a commitment made concrete in the Creed and Universal Prayer. We cannot afford to take what we say/sing lightly!

To Ponder

- I might emphasize the direct address at the beginning and end of the Gospel proclamation by . . .

- Realizing that Christ is present in the very proclamation of the Gospel urges, inspires, commands me to . . .

Prayer

Ever-present God,
we glorify you, we praise you, we adore you
    in the word you speak to us.
May we acclaim with full throat your Son's Divine Presence.
Help us not only to hear the Gospel,
but to take it into our very being as Jesus Christ's Life-giving Presence.
Strengthen us to live what we hear
so that all our actions are consistent with Jesus' life.
May we witness to our commitment to do your holy will in all things.
We ask this through Christ our Lord. Amen.

1.7   I BELIEVE IN

Roman Missal Text

I believe in one God,
the Father almighty,
maker of heaven and earth,
of all things visible and invisible.

I believe in one Lord Jesus Christ,
the Only Begotten Son of God,
born of the Father before all ages.
God from God, Light from Light,
true God from true God,
begotten, not made, consubstantial with the Father;
through him all things were made.
For us men and for our salvation
he came down from heaven,
and by the Holy Spirit was incarnate of the Virgin Mary,
and became man.

For our sake he was crucified under Pontius Pilate,
he suffered death and was buried,
and rose again on the third day
in accordance with the Scriptures.
He ascended into heaven
and is seated at the right hand of the Father.
He will come again in glory
to judge the living and the dead
and his kingdom will have no end.

I believe in the Holy Spirit, the Lord, the giver of life,
who proceeds from the Father and the Son,
who with the Father and the Son is adored and glorified,
who has spoken through the prophets.

I believe in one, holy, catholic and apostolic Church.
I confess one Baptism for the forgiveness of sins
and I look forward to the resurrection of the dead
and the life of the world to come. Amen.

—no. 18

Reflection

I believe . . . I believe . . . I believe . . . I believe. Four times, we profess, "I believe." The present translation reflects the Latin *Credo*, first person singular: I believe. While as the Body of Christ our belief is a collective one (as one Body we all hold the same truths), from early times creeds have called for a *personal* profession. Which also calls forth from us a *personal* response.

Each occurrence of "I believe" is followed by the preposition *in*. This little, two-letter word can suggest many things to us. Being *in* means that we are "within"—surrounded, enclosed, contained. The *in* is fourfold: Father, Jesus Christ, Holy Spirit, Church. We profess that we are one with Father, Jesus Christ, Holy Spirit, and Church. And we must remember that Church is not institution or building, but a Person, the Body of Christ. I believe "in" means that our belief is entirely relational. Our belief places us in a unique kinship with the Three Persons of God—through Baptism, we become God's children, we are in a love-relationship with God, and we are in a Life-relationship with God. We live out this relationship in the Church, the Body of Christ. Church—each other being one in Christ— makes visible the divine relating to which we are called. "I believe in God and Church" is not a matter of passive content, but is active relating.

I believe "in" can also suggest inclusion or involvement. Our "in group" is the Divine Persons! Our "I believe" is not so much a matter of intellectual assent as it is personal commitment to a way of life shown us by Jesus Christ. Our profession includes a devotedness to our common identity such that we embrace and witness to all that we hear time after time in the proclamation of the Gospel. Our "I believe" is a commitment to live the Gospel.

In the Creed, we profess something essential about each of the Three Persons of the Holy Trinity as well as of the Church. Father: Creator. Jesus Christ: so much one with the Father that he is the Divine Word through which all is created, he was made flesh by the power of the Holy Spirit, he is our Savior, risen from the dead; he continues his saving ministry until the end of time, when he will return to gather all back to the Father. Holy Spirit: source of Life and holiness, the personification of the love of the Father and Son, origin of wisdom and truth. Church: one Body under Christ her Head, universally continuing Jesus' saving ministry, built up through baptismal membership making visible Christ's promise of forgiveness and eternal Life.

The power of this profession must be expressed through strong voices that carry our conviction. It will not do to mumble half-heartedly through these words. They give credence to who we are in Christ and to the call to live as he did.

To Ponder

- I believe in . . . , for . . . , because . . .
- My profession of faith comes most alive when I . . .
- I am aware of living this profession when . . .

Prayer

Almighty God,
we adore and glorify you for your greatness and goodness,
for giving us the gift of faith and salvation,
and for inviting us to share in the privilege of your Life and holiness.
As we profess our belief in your three Divine Persons and the Church,
strengthen us so that these words become a way of living for us,
imbue us with enthusiasm for deepening our relationship with you,
and instill in us a great love for this Church whom we make visible
as we gather to adore and glorify your majesty and splendor.
We ask this through Christ our Lord. Amen.

1.8   BLESSED ARE YOU . . .

Roman Missal Text

> Blessed are you, Lord God of all creation,
> for through your goodness we have received
> the bread we offer you:
> fruit of the earth and work of human hands,
> it will become for us the bread of life.
>
> —no. 23

> Blessed are you, Lord God of all creation,
> for through your goodness we have received
> the wine we offer you:
> fruit of the vine and work of human hands,
> it will become our spiritual drink.
>
> —no. 25

Reflection

At Sunday Mass we rarely hear these two beautiful prayers because we are usually singing a hymn during the Presentation and Preparation of the Gifts and Altar. These prayers place us in the tradition of our Jewish heritage—they are based on Jewish meal prayers called *berakoth*, "blessings." Note that these two prayers begin with our blessing God: "Blessed are you, Lord God." Many of us grew up with (and still use) the traditional Catholic meal prayer:

> Bless us, O Lord, and these thy gifts,
> which we are about to receive from thy bounty,
> through Christ our Lord. Amen.

Notice the difference. In our present liturgical text, we bless God; in our devotional meal prayer, we ask God to bless us. Our Eucharistic meal prayer praises (blesses) God for the gifts we have been given. But so much more is being said in these two beautiful prayers.

First, we qualify "Lord God" as Creator and the one whose goodness provides us with these gifts. The bread and wine are not only the "fruit of the earth" and "fruit of the vine," but also the "work of human hands." God's gifts are not placed on the altar as creation gave them to us, but as manipulated by our own hands into something more nourishing and satisfying than the fruits even creation gives us. These words suggest to us that we cooperate with God's continual act of creation. God gives us gifts in pure form, so to speak, and we fashion them into another form that is more suited to human use and our liturgical purpose. Isn't it wonderful how God uses us finite humans to take natural gifts and recreate them?

Second, the prayers make clear that the gifts we present during the Eucharistic liturgy are gifts we "have received." Everything we have and are is a gift from God. Even the bread and wine we present to become the very Body and Blood of the divine, risen Son originates as a gift from God. The gifts we offer God are truly not our own, but gifts given us. In our poverty of spirit we receive from God what we intend to offer back to God. God is a God of goodness and gifts.

Third, the bread and wine "will become for us" (curiously, the "for us" is omitted in the prayer over the chalice) "the bread of life" and our "spiritual drink." These gifts are intended for a very specific purpose: to be offered to God so that the divine action can change them from mere fruit of the earth/vine to the sublime Gift of the risen Son's very Body and Blood. They also change us. These gifts are intended for our Holy Communion, which continues its fruits in our ongoing communion with God and each other.

Fourth, St. Paul, in speaking of the glory about to be revealed to us in Christ Jesus, also includes creation that "will be set free from its bondage . . . and will obtain the freedom of the glory of the children of God" (Romans 8:21). Both creation and we are "groaning in labor pains" as we await "the redemption of our bodies" (Romans 8:22–23). Creation, too, shares in the promised fullness of Christ's saving work. Creation, with us, comes to fullness in Christ. Wheat and grapes, changed by our labors into bread and wine, are changed into that for which we groan: the very Body and Blood of the risen Christ.

Fifth, the rubrics accompanying these prayers has the priest saying them standing at the altar with the bread and wine "slightly raised." At the conclusion of each prayer, the bread and wine are then placed on the altar. Being "slightly raised" heightens the gifts' being placed on the altar. They will be the continual sacrifice of Christ's self-giving. Because these gifts are also the work of our hands, we ourselves are united with the bread and wine. We ourselves are placed on the altar. We ourselves are joined to Christ's continual sacrifice of self-giving. We ourselves are readied to be transformed by God into more perfect members of the Divine Son's Body.

To Ponder

- I cooperate with God in recreating creation when I . . .

- I thwart the beauty of creation when I . . .

- I am most inclined to place myself on the altar along with the bread and wine when I . . .

Prayer

Blessed are you, Lord God of all creation,
for you have given us all good things
and have invited us to cooperate with you
in bringing all of creation to the fullness of redemption.
May our praise of you be constant
even as we labor to use your gifts for the good of all.
May we be ever so willing to join ourselves with Christ in his life of
total love and self-giving.
We ask this through Christ our Lord. Amen.

1.9   CHRIST . . . HUMBLED HIMSELF

Roman Missal Text

By the mystery of this water and wine
may we come to share in the divinity of Christ
who humbled himself to share in our humanity.

—no. 24

Reflection

When we become familiar enough with the liturgical texts, we begin to notice cross-references—that is, how a text used in one place is borrowed from another. This is very true for this text given for our reflection. Let us pause now to pray the Collect from the Mass during the Day for the Nativity of the Lord [Christmas]:

O God, who wonderfully created the dignity of human nature / and still more wonderfully restored it, / grant, we pray, / that we may share in the divinity of Christ, / who humbled himself to share in our humanity. / Who lives and reigns with you in the unity of the Holy Spirit, one God, for ever and ever.

Here are the words in both texts: " . . . [may we come to] share in the divinity of Christ, who humbled himself to share in our humanity." We pray ourselves into the mystery of the Incarnation! While the mixing of the water and wine symbolizes the human and divine natures of Christ, so does this also symbolize our being taken up into Christ's life through Baptism; it symbolizes our sharing in the very Divine life of the risen Christ.

The fuller mystery of Christmas is captured not simply in Christ's emptying himself of his divinity to be "born in human likeness" (Philippians 2:7), not simply in Christ's descending from heaven to earth, but also by his Incarnation the opposite movement is made possible for us. We ourselves ascend from earth to heaven to share in the promise of the fullness of Life. Christmas is as much a feast about our rebirth in Christ as it is about Christ's birth into humanity. Unfortunately, the priest prays this prayer "quietly," so we never hear it, unless we can overhear it at a weekday Mass when there is no music. Therefore, we miss the power of what is being prayed. In effect, every Mass is a reminder of the Incarnation. Every Mass is a kind of celebration of Christmas, where we are immersed in the awesome mystery of Christ's becoming incarnate.

The Collect for the daytime Mass on Christmas includes a line not in the words spoken quietly at the commingling of water and wine. The Collect reminds us of our dignity as human beings made in the image and likeness of God, and God's mercy and graciousness in overlooking our human weakness continually to restore this wondrous dignity. God gifts us with "a share in the divinity of Christ." What a great thing to celebrate at each Mass! Christ "humbled himself," and we are raised up in dignity and splendor. Christ's humility becomes our glory!

To Ponder

- Sharing in Christ's divinity means to me . . .

- The dignity I've received from the Creator means to me . . .

Prayer

Gracious God,
you have bestowed on us a great dignity
    by being created in your very image and likeness.
And then with the coming of Christ incarnate,
you give us even more, a share in your very divinity.
May we always preserve this grace given us,
nurture it so that we can witness more fully your Presence among us,
and build each other up as members of the Body of Christ.
We ask this through Christ our Lord. Amen.

1.10   AT THE SAVIOR'S COMMAND . . .

Roman Missal Text

> At the Savior's command
> and formed by divine teaching,
> we dare to say:

> —no. 124

Reflection

Each of the three short lines of the invitation to pray the Our Father carries a different idea. How much can be packed in a few words!

At the Savior's command: these are not just nice words we are saying in the Our Father. They were not only given us by the Savior himself (see Matthew 6:9–13; Luke 11:2–4), but commanded that they be said. A very early Church document (possibly contemporaneous with the New Testament itself) called the *Didache* records the earliest Church precept we have concerning prayer: Christians are to pray the Our Father three times daily (*Didache*, 8:3). Not just once, but three times daily are we to pray this prayer!

In The Lord's Prayer, we are reminded of Jesus' own way of relating to God and other. He calls God "Father," avowing a progenitive relationship, a relationship of Life given and received. Jesus himself is the Only-Begotten Son. And when we call God "Our Father," we avow our own relationship to God as beloved daughters and sons, brothers and sisters in Christ. It is good for us to remember multiple times daily that our Life and being are gifts from God, that God desires to be in intimate relationship with us, and that God cares for us and loves us into Life. Our response to Jesus' command to pray as he taught us is an act witnessing to our choice to receive the gifts of Life and love, holiness and goodness, sustenance and protection, forgiveness and mercy given us by a God who invites us into a most astounding relationship with our Creator.

formed by divine teaching: the words of the Our Father are made concrete in the very Life and being of the Word made Flesh. Jesus showed us how to make holy God's name by showing us how to pray often. He showed us how to do the Father's will by being ever obedient—even when his fidelity led to suffering and death on the cross. He showed us how to nourish others and ourselves by often being at meals, by multiplying the loaves and fish for the hungry crowd, by giving us his very Body and Blood as our heavenly food. He showed us how to heal and forgive, even his executioners (see Luke 23:34). More than this, Jesus' life forms us in a way of life. The whole Gospel shows us that what God wills for us is fullness of Life. Our destiny is to be with our Father in heaven. Jesus taught us well. Let us learn well.

we dare to say: Even when taught how to pray by Jesus, we are still very bold to address our God. Any hesitation is erased by Jesus' command to pray thus, and by remaining in a deep and loving relationship with God. We dare, are encouraged and emboldened, to pray most surely when we live the way of life Jesus taught us. For this is how we grow in our intimate relationship with God. We speak to our Creator because Jesus has shown us the way and invited us to do so. Our boldness does not come from our own efforts, but from the gifts that God has already given us, especially the gifts of faith, hope, and love. This *dare to pray* as Jesus taught us carries no defiant challenge (as when children dare each other to do something risky or seemingly beyond their strength or ability), but instead it is a dare inviting us to prove our courage to live the Gospel.

This invitation to pray the Lord's Prayer is not made of empty words. It invites and challenges us to mean what we say, to live what we mean.

To Ponder

- My intimate relationship with God is expressed daily when I . . .

- My boldness in prayer leads me to . . .

Prayer

How bold we are, Creator God,
to dare to address you intimately in prayer!
How encouraged we are, Creator God,
when we make our needs known to you!
You hear and answer all our prayers
and form us more perfectly in your Divine Image
    when we open our hearts to you.
Teach us to pray more often and with greater fervor
that we might live more perfectly
the Gospel instruction your Son has revealed to us.
We ask this through Christ our Lord. Amen.

1.11 ALL IS GOD'S . . .

Roman Missal Text

> For the kingdom,
> the power and the glory are yours
> now and for ever.
>
> —no. 125

Reflection

This doxology (a short formula of praise to God) has never been part of our devotional, Catholic praying of the Our Father. Nor is it part of either of the Our Father texts as given in the Gospels of Matthew and Luke. But it has from early on been included in the Mass formula for the Lord's Prayer, after the embolism (textual insertion), that asks God to "Deliver us . . . from evil." The impetus for concluding the Lord's Prayer with the doxology comes from that early Church document the *Didache*, where the words concluding the Our Father are "for yours is the power and glory forever" (*Didache*, 8:2).

We live in a democratic republic, so the notion of kingdom is not part of our heritage. God's Kingdom, however, is not marked by lands and subjects, wealth and domination, but rather by peace and mercy for all who do God's holy will. God's Kingdom, then, is present wherever people are obedient to God's will and open to God's offer of Life. God's Kingdom is a state of relationship between God and us, and us among ourselves. It is a relationship that reflects the loving community of the Triune God. The power that belongs to God, our King, is not a domination over, but a potency to bring forth Life and goodness. God is not simply a passive, benevolent King. God guides and strengthens us to cooperate with the divine power to bring about a reign of peace and justice, forgiveness and mercy, care and love.

We sang God's glory at the beginning of Mass. We say again just before we receive Holy Communion that all glory and praise belong to God "now and forever." God's glory is the trace of Divine Presence in our midst. This Presence is not simply what we anticipate in heaven after our human death. There in heaven, yes, we will have the fullness of God's Life and be immersed in the wonder of God's full glory revealed to us. But already now, as we faithfully live the Gospel, we encounter God's Life and glory. Our own joy at making right choices, bringing happiness to others, forgiving when wronged, sharing what has been given to us with others, healing through our own touch and presence those who are hurting in any way is a trace of God's glory. We encounter God's glory—the trace of Divine Presence in our midst—and then are privileged to bring that glory to others.

To Ponder

- I bring about the Presence of God's Kingdom in these ways . . .

- I exercise the power of God to . . .

- I reveal God's Presence, God's glory to others when I . . .

Prayer

We ever praise you, O glorious God, for your Presence to us.
Your power lifts us up to live as Jesus did
and thus brings your Presence to all those we meet
    in the simple everyday acts we do.
May we always give you praise for your gift of Life
and abundance of good gifts you shower upon us.
May we willingly share those gifts with others
and bring you glory now and forever.
We ask this through Christ our Lord. Amen.

1.12 PEACE I GIVE YOU

Roman Missal Text

Lord Jesus Christ,
who said to your Apostles:
Peace I leave you, my peace I give you,
look not on our sins,
but on the faith of your Church,
and graciously grant her peace and unity
in accordance with your will.
Who live and reign for ever and ever.

—no. 126

The peace of the Lord be with you always.

—no. 127

Let us offer each other the sign of peace.

—no. 128

Reflection

Peace I leave you, my peace I give you. What a gift! What comforting words! This peace was not only given to the Apostles in the Upper Room after the Resurrection, but is given to each of us through the Holy Spirit we receive at Baptism. Further, this peace is not the peace of human making, but the Life-giving peace of the risen Christ. These words, which we hear at every Mass, are the words of the risen Christ to the disciples (see Luke 24:36; John 20:19, 21, 26).

We usually think of peace as the absence of tension and strife, war and domination. This is the peace of human making, which happens when we act "in accordance with [God's] will." When we put our own will first, we dominate others and bring anything but peace. When we act "in accordance with [God's] will," we not only are the agents of peace among those we encounter, but we also continue the risen Christ's desire for peace and unity among all peoples. Acting "in accordance with [God's] will" is nothing less than living the Gospel, than living as Jesus did. We are given the Holy Spirit to bring this Life-giving peace to our world.

The peace of the Lord be with you always. Such a gracious gift the risen Christ gives us! Perhaps the key word of this gift is *always*. Peace is not something that comes and goes. The habit of peace-making flows from the kind of relationship we have with Christ. Our habit of peace comes from our doing as St. Paul did: "I have been crucified with Christ; and it is no longer I who live, but it is Christ who lives in me" (Galatians 2:19–20). To be crucified with Christ means that we are as self-giving for others as he was. The faith of the Church is visible in our self-giving. The faith of the Church grows through our care and love of others. The faith of the Church means that we get out of the way so Christ can take hold of us, and our way of living, and form us into ever more faithful disciples.

Let us offer each other the sign of peace. Having heard the comforting words of the gift of peace from the risen Christ, we are invited to share that peace with each other: This is not a social time! This exchange of peace is a sacred time when we give to each other the gift we have been given. It is a sign of faith and unity in our common identity as the Body of Christ. This is why it is not necessary to give the Sign of Peace to everyone at Mass, but only to those immediately around us. To extend peace to a few of the Body of Christ is symbolic of extending it to all the Body of Christ. This sign is an acknowledgment that we are the Body of Christ and our life is about striving to be faithful members of that Body.

Sometimes we call this the "kiss" of peace. This language points to the custom of how the Sign of Peace was once exchanged[3] and from a gesture the presider used to do before exchanging the Sign of Peace with other ministers at a solemn High Mass (at a time when the sharing of peace was seldom if ever done among the assembly members). The priest would kiss the altar before exchanging peace with another minister. He does this same gesture at the beginning and end of Mass. The altar is consecrated with Holy Chrism, making it a sign of the Presence of Christ in our midst. This is why the altar is always central to our liturgical celebrations. When the Kiss of Peace originated with kissing the altar, it was even more clear that it is Christ's peace that is exchanged. The priest no longer kisses the altar before the invitation to offer peace to each other in the Body of Christ. But it is always good to remember that the source of the peace we offer each other is Christ, whose gift to us is the Holy Spirit of peace.

To Ponder

- If I think of the Sign of Peace as the gift of the Holy Spirit given me in the risen Christ, this sign becomes for me . . .

- When I become aware of choosing God's will over my own, the peace I experience is . . .

---

3. In some cultures, the gesture of a kiss is a more universal greeting than in our own.

Prayer

God of peace and reconciliation,
your Holy Spirit gives us your peace as a gift to share with one another.
May we exchange this sign with integrity and good will.
May the Sign of Peace strengthen us to choose your will over our own.
May the Sign of Peace bring unity and good will
to all the encounters I have with others during my daily living.
We ask this through Christ our Lord. Amen.

1.13 BEHOLD THE LAMB OF GOD

Roman Missal Text

Behold the Lamb of God,
behold him who takes away the sins of the world.
Blessed are those called to the supper of the Lamb.

Lord, I am not worthy
that you should enter under my roof,
but only say the word
and my soul shall be healed.

—no. 132

Reflection

In the most recent translation of *The Roman Missal*, the allusions to Scripture are more evident. In the invitation to Holy Communion and the assembly's response to that invitation, we have four Scripture references, which help us to delve more deeply into the meaning of what we are about as we receive Christ's Body and Blood.

The first Scripture reference occurs in the first word of the invitation: "Behold." It actually occurs twice. *Behold* is the English translation of the Latin *ecce*, which underscores the importance of the salutation. "Behold" occurs three times in the Lukan Incarnation account. Gabriel addresses Mary twice with "Behold." The first time, to get her attention that she will conceive by the Holy Spirit (see Luke 1:31). The second time, to alert her to the sign that God will accomplish these wondrous deeds in her elderly cousin Elizabeth, who is also carrying a child (see Luke 1:36). "Behold" occurs a third time, when Mary responds to Gabriel saying that she is God's handmaid and will do as God asks (Luke 1:38). In all three instances, the "Behold" serves to alert us to something extraordinary happening. When we hear "Behold" before Holy Communion, we are also alerted that something extraordinary is happening.

The second Scripture reference is the title Lamb of God. John the Baptist gives this title to Jesus when he announces to his disciples Jesus' Presence: "Behold, the Lamb of God, who takes away the sin of the world" (John 1:29). We have here also the exclamation "Behold." John is calling attention to Jesus as the Lamb of God, as the One who would give over his life for us. Jesus' self-giving is visible in his giving himself to the disciples at the Last Supper under the signs of bread and wine, in his death on the cross, in his continual self-giving to us in the Eucharist. Holy Communion is a great gift of nourishment, at the same time it is a pledge of the risen Christ's continued self-giving and a call to us to respond with the same self-giving.

The third Scripture reference occurs in the final words of the invitation: "Blessed are those called to the supper of the Lamb" (see Revelation 19:9). The NRSVCE[4] renders this line the "marriage supper," while the NABRE[5] translates the phrase as "wedding feast." Both translations emphasize unity and joy, and both remind us of the Messianic Banquet that takes place eternally before the throne of the Lamb. Christ is our Bridegroom and invites us to intimate union with him. Our Holy Communion is already a participation in the fullness of Life that is to come. Surely, we are blessed by receiving the Heavenly Food that is the very Body and Blood of the divine, risen Son.

The fourth Scripture reference occurs in the assembly response. It is a slight paraphrase ("soul" rather than "servant," for example) of the response of the centurion to Jesus in the Gospel story about the healing of the centurion's servant. In fact, the centurion himself does not even personally address Jesus; he sends friends to say this to Jesus as Jesus nears the house where the servant is ill, such is the centurion's great respect and humility (see Luke 7:6–10). Such ought to be our attitude as we approach to receive the Body and Blood of Christ. The healing requested by the centurion for his servant was physical healing; Jesus granted his request and the servant returned to health. *Healing* and *health* here remind us that these words in Hebrew mean "salvation." When we respond asking that our "soul shall be healed," we are indicating our desire that receiving Holy Communion leads us to salvation, to eternal Life. This response places us in a salvation/eschatological context where we express our yearning to be with the Lord Jesus forever in heaven. This is the ultimate healing. Our expression of unworthiness, beyond humility, is an acknowledgment of the relationship we have with Christ—he is the Divine One who calls us, nevertheless, into Divine Presence and nourishes us with his very self.

So much to this invitation and response to receive Holy Communion! So much being given us! So much being demanded of us! May we always approach Holy Communion with the humility, reverence, and awe that the risen Christ's self-giving deserves!

---

4. *New Revised Standard Version: Catholic Edition*
5. *New American Bible, Revised Edition*

To Ponder

- When I hear myself being invited to the "supper of the Lamb," I am stirred to . . .

- The healing-salvation that Holy Communion always brings is . . .

Prayer

Eternal Father,
having triumphed over death and risen to new life,
the Lamb of God now sits at your right hand.
As the risen Christ continues to give himself to us as heavenly Food,
may we be nourished and strengthened
to respond by our own self-giving to others.
We ask this through Christ our Lord. Amen.

1.14   AMEN

Roman Missal Text

> The Body of Christ. Amen. (no. 134)
> The Blood of Christ. Amen.

Reflection

Amen. So be it. Yes! It is so. This Hebrew word can be said many ways, but they all come down to affirmation and commitment. We often say Amen without too much or even any thought. It ends our prayers, so we just say it. It's habit. The challenge is to make this habit become an ongoing affirmation of our own identity as Body of Christ.

The rubric indicates that the Communion minister (priest, deacon, extraordinary minister) shows the consecrated bread and/or the consecrated wine to the communicant. He or she is to raise the Host or Cup slightly, saying "The Body of Christ" or "The Blood of Christ." Our Amen is really a double faith acclamation. We say Amen to the Real Presence of the risen Christ in the consecrated Bread and Wine. Christ is really our Heavenly Food. We truly take the Body and Blood of the risen Christ and consume it. It is to this reality that we say Amen. It is a faith statement made visible in our word but also in our action of taking and eating and drinking.

But something else is being said in our Amen. At Baptism, we were made members of the Body of Christ. His risen Body is present in many modes: in the Church gathered for liturgy, in the consecrated Bread and Wine, in the Scriptures proclaimed, and in each member of the Body of Christ (*Constitution on the Sacred Liturgy*, no. 7). We ourselves are a real Presence. So, our Amen is not only affirming the Real Presence of Christ in the Eucharistic species, it is also an affirmation of our own Baptismal identity as the Body of Christ. The Body of Christ receives the Body of Christ. The Body of Christ is his continued risen Presence in our midst.

Long ago St. Augustine recognized this double reality, this double Presence of the risen Christ. In a now well-known passage from his *Sermon 272*, he makes this startling statement:

> If you are to understand what it means to be the Body of Christ, hear what Paul has to say: "Now you are the Body of Christ and individually members of it" (1 Corinthians 12:27). If you are the Body of Christ and members of it, then it is that mystery which is placed on the Lord's Table: you receive the mystery, which is to say the Body of Christ, your very self. You answer "Amen" to who you are and in the answer, you embrace yourself. You hear, Body of Christ, and answer Amen. Be a member of Christ's Body, that your Amen will be true.[6]

Amazing! The mystery of ourselves is placed on the altar along with the bread and wine. Amazing! We are transformed by eating and drinking the Body and Blood of Christ. Amazing! We receive ourselves. This same sentiment is echoed in the Prayer after Communion on August 28, the Memorial of St. Augustine: "May partaking of Christ's table / sanctify us, we pray, O Lord, / that, being made members of his Body, / we may become what we have received. / Through Christ our Lord."

St. Augustine is also giving us a caution: we must live the mystery of the reality of our identity as the Body of Christ. It is not enough to say Amen and then not live as Jesus did, not live the Gospel. The way we live confirms our belief in the Real Presence. If our words are to be true, then our Amen must be carried forth in our daily living. Receiving Holy Communion makes a difference in our behavior, in how we relate to others, in how we are able to love others with more depth and conviction. Our daily living makes our Amen true or false. Amazing! Our Amen makes a difference.

---

6. Author's translation

To Ponder

- What strikes me most about the lines from St. Augustine's sermon is . . .

- What challenges me the most is . . .

- Holy Communion is never simply a private act; it always nudges me to reach out to others in these ways . . .

Prayer

Amazing God, your Son, Jesus Christ,
has given us the Gift of his very Body and Blood
   for our strength and nourishment.
As we say Amen to his Divine Presence,
may we say Amen to our commitment to live the Gospel
as he commanded and lead others to this great Banquet of Love,
which he has given us.
We ask this through Christ our Lord. Amen.

1.15   GO . . . THANKS

Roman Missal Text

Go forth, the Mass is ended. Thanks be to God.
Or
Go and announce the Gospel of the Lord. Thanks be to God.
Or
Go in peace, glorifying the Lord by your life. Thanks be to God.
Or
Go in peace. Thanks be to God.

—no. 144

Reflection

No matter which choice the deacon or priest uses for the Dismissal at the end of Mass, the Dismissals all begin with a key word: *Go.* Yes, we are to leave the church building and each other as an assembly before the Lord and return to our daily living. However, there is more happening here than simply leave-taking. We are dismissed, to be sure; but we are dismissed with a commission to live the Mystery we have celebrated, to live the Gospel, to live Jesus' self-giving. This dismissal is so important for Eucharistic living that we repeat this text with a new reflection at 5.15. It serves as a kind of conclusion, as a way of sending the user of this book to "Go forth."

When we are told by the deacon or priest to "Go forth, the Mass in ended," we are not being told to forget about the celebration in which we have just participated and get out and get on with our lives. Yes, the Mass as a ritual celebration is ended. It begins in the name of the Trinity with the Sign of the Cross, and it ends with a blessing during which we make the Sign of the Cross. The ritual unfolds in time and space, has a beginning and ending. But, no, the Eucharistic Mystery does not end; it continues beyond the walls of the building and the assembly of people who have gathered. Being the Body of Christ continues as we leave the sacred space and take up our daily activities.

The middle two Dismissal formulas were chosen by Pope Benedict XVI himself to be included in *The Roman Missal*, third edition, to make even more clear to us that we are dismissed to live what we have celebrated. No one who reads what the Holy Father has written about liturgy can miss an underlying agenda. He is very concerned that the Mass not simply end with the ritual or that we leave its significance behind as we go back to our busy lives. Pope Benedict was very emphatic about our coming to a deeper understanding that Eucharist is a Mystery to be lived. What we have celebrated we take into our homes and neighborhoods, workplaces and play places, to family and strangers, and make it visible by the way we live the Gospel values Jesus has taught us.

We "announce the Gospel" of the Lord not by standing on a street corner and reading a Gospel to passersby. Actually, this would be an easy way out of the demands made upon us in our participation in the Eucharistic liturgy. What this imperative statement means is that we announce the Gospel by living consistently with the values that Jesus has given us. In a real sense, this means that our lives are countercultural signs that our true home is not here. We journey in this life toward the fullness of Life that will one day be given to the faithful members of the Body of Christ. This task is not an easy one! But gaining fullness of Life is worth whatever is demanded by the Eucharist—dying to self and living like Christ.

We "glorify the Lord by [our] life" not by kneeling in prayer all the time, although daily prayer is essential if we are to grow in our graced relationship with God and each other. We give God glory, yes, in prayer, liturgy, and other kinds of celebrations and observances such as doing penance on Fridays and during Lent. But sometimes we forget that the good choices we make every day glorify God. Sometimes we forget that fulfilling our duties in life with a happy disposition gives God glory. Sometimes we forget that caring and loving others gives God glory. Our very lives glorify God when they are lived according to Gospel values, when they reflect the presence of the risen Christ in our midst.

The simplest of the four Dismissal formulas is the last one: "Go in peace." Its simplicity can fool us. What is the peace we are to take with us? It is the same peace we exchanged at the Sign of Peace—that is, the peace of the Christ who dwells within each of us. To "Go in peace" means that we go forth with a full commitment to be Christ for others. Anything less than being faithful disciples means that we are sowing seeds of discord rather than peace. To "Go in peace" means that we return to our daily living with a much deeper appreciation for the gift of being Body of Christ, his very Presence, for all those we meet. Go in peace challenges us to accept our Baptismal identity and live it to the fullest.

Our response to each of the Dismissal formulas is "Thanks be to God." Our hearts can be filled with gratitude for many things at the conclusion of Mass. We are grateful for the gift of hearing God's Word, for the gift of God's Spirit transforming the bread and wine into Christ's risen Body and Blood, for the gift of sharing with each other an opportunity to sing God's praises, for the time to make our needs known to a caring and compassionate God, to name a few. Perhaps mostly, though, our hearts are filled with the Presence of the Divine Son within us, and for this we are most thankful. We are thankful for the privilege of being baptized members of the Body of Christ who are sent forth to live what we have been given. We are thankful for our own growth in holiness that will bring us the fullness of Life eternal.

To Ponder

- What I find common among the four Dismissal formulas is . . . How they differ is . . .
- The dismissal I prefer is . . . because . . .

Prayer

We are your pilgrim Church, loving God,
who is given the Gift of your Son's Body and Blood
so that we can more perfectly be the Body of Christ for others.
In the midst of the demands and challenges of our daily living,
help us to remember all you have given us
and to have ever grateful hearts for the Eucharistic Mystery,
which continues your Son's saving work among us and through us.
We ask this through Christ our Lord. Amen.

CHAPTER 2

TEXTS DRAWN FROM THE COLLECTS

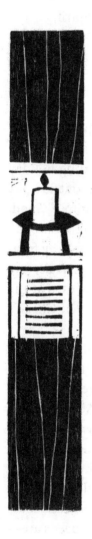

The word *collect* is new to the third edition of *The Roman Missal*, but not to the language of our Eucharistic liturgy. It was used in earlier Mass books. *Collect* refers to the first of the three presidential prayers (the other two being the Prayer over the Offerings and the Prayer after Communion). In the previous *Sacramentary*, the Collect was called "Opening Prayer." Changing the name helps us understand more clearly that the prayer given in *The Roman Missal* is not the whole opening prayer, but is the conclusion to it. It "collects" together the individual prayers of everyone at the Eucharistic liturgy—of all of us who pray in the depths of our hearts during the silence after the invitation "Let us pray."

The Collects are rich in theological content and filled with beautiful imagery. Often they help us understand a feast or season. We turn now to some of that excellent prayer language.

2.1 Run Forth to Meet Your Christ

Roman Missal Text

> Grant your faithful, we pray, almighty God,
> the resolve to run forth to meet your Christ
> with righteous deeds at his coming,
> so that, gathered at his right hand,
> they may be worthy to possess the heavenly Kingdom.
> Through our Lord Jesus Christ, your Son,
> who lives and reigns with you in the unity of the Holy Spirit,
> one God, for ever and ever. Amen.
>
> —Collect, First Sunday of Advent

Reflection

Long, long before Advent (the liturgical season which prepares us for the coming of Christ), the marketplace is pounding away at us to prepare for Christmas—by buying toys and other gifts, by buying and sending holiday cards, by buying various kinds of decorations for both inside and outside our homes. Buy, buy, buy: that is the message. Some of us might even think, "Good. Advent is finally here, and we can 'officially' begin our Christmas preparations." Hopefully, the beginning of Advent is a turning point for us—turning away from busyness toward a greater quiet with focus on Christ. This Collect turns us, too; surprisingly, though, not toward celebration of the past coming of Jesus at the first Christmas, but instead toward a future event that is not here yet: Christ's Second Coming.

After Jesus predicted his passion and death and the persecutions that would take place, he assured the disciples that he would return in great power (see Matthew 24:29–30; Mark 13:24–27; Luke 21:25–28). We commonly refer to this as Jesus' Second Coming. So when this Collect for the First Sunday of Advent speaks of Christ's coming, it is not pointing us toward Christmas, but toward a future event not yet here, Christ's Second Coming. Further, this prayer also tells us how we are to be in this time between Christ's First Coming at his birth into human life and his Second Coming that heralds our eternal birth into the fullness of Life.

We are reminded that we are to meet our Christ with "righteous deeds at his coming." Matthew's Gospel has Jesus telling us what these righteous deeds are—those deeds accomplished by the blessed who "inherit the kingdom prepared for [us] from the foundation of the world" (Matthew 25:34): feeding the hungry, giving drink to the thirsty, clothing the naked, caring for those who are ill, visiting the imprisoned. Jesus teaches us that when we do these acts of mercy and kindness for "one of the least of these who are members of [his] family," we do it for him (Matthew 25:40). Righteous deeds are the way we reach out to others as Jesus has reached out to us. They are the conduct of those who know themselves to be the Body of Christ and who strive to live as Jesus did. Righteous deeds are those that deepen our relationship with God and others. The cement that binds us together is the Presence of the risen Christ within and among us.

When our lives are spent in doing righteous deeds, then Christ's Second Coming holds no fear for us. Instead, we eagerly anticipate his coming because he will bring to fulfillment all things. The image in this Collect is quite beautiful: we are to "resolve to run forth to meet [our] Christ." Resolve: resolutely, courageously, unhesitatingly set on a course of life that is Gospel living. When a need is presented, we eagerly reach out to the other because we have developed a habit of recognizing Christ in the other. Our resolution to act is not a product of dogged determination no matter what, but is a product of the love exchange between Christ and us and between others and us. We reach out to others because we strive to love as Jesus did. And so we "run forth to meet [our] Christ." We don't saunter, we don't walk, we don't take detours. We *run* forth to meet Christ—not simply at the end of time, but here and now to the person in need. For that person is Christ.

To Ponder

- My Advent is characterized by my "resolve to run forth to meet Christ" when I . . . This makes a difference in how I view Christmas in that . . .

- The person in need I tend to neglect is . . . The person in need I run forth to help is . . .

Prayer

Almighty God,
you come to us in many ways and through many persons.
Help us to see the Presence of your Divine Son
    in each of the situations and persons we encounter each day.
May we grow in responding as Jesus would to those who are in need.
May we prepare for Christmas
by opening our lives more perfectly to the presence of others.
We ask this through Christ our Lord. Amen.

2.2   Pour Forth Grace

Roman Missal Text

> Pour forth, we beseech you, O Lord,
> your grace into our hearts,
> that we, to whom the Incarnation of Christ your Son
> was made known by the message of an Angel,
> may by his Passion and Cross
> be brought to the glory of his Resurrection.
> Who lives and reigns with you in the unity of the Holy Spirit,
> one God, for ever and ever. Amen.
>
> —Collect, Fourth Sunday of Advent

Reflection

On this, the last Sunday of Advent and before Christmas, we pray a Collect that is very familiar to many of us who heard (and sometimes still hear) church bells ring at six o'clock in the morning, at noon, and at six o'clock in the evening, calling us to pray the Angelus. This popular devotion accompanying the ringing of bells is truly a joyous Christmas prayer that we have traditionally prayed three times daily throughout the year. It's as though we wanted to make every day Christmas! The prayer recalls for us Gabriel's visit to Mary to announce that she would conceive by the Holy Spirit; it recalls Mary's fiat, her yes response to God's singular request of her; it recalls Jesus' birth, the Word made flesh who dwells among us. This is the mystery of Presence for which we have been preparing during Advent. This is the mystery of Presence that distinguishes us as the Body of Christ who shares in the Divine Life and salvation that Jesus came to offer us.

Pour forth . . . your grace. What we beseech God is for God's very Life to be showered upon us ever more abundantly. We don't merely ask, nor beg, nor coax—we beseech, we cry out with urgency, with expectation, with hope. God's gift of Life to us—begun at Baptism—is a continual outpouring of God's love for us. Because it is totally undeserved, God's Life is ever more the pure gift. God's will is that we share in the Divine Life. By opening ourselves to this Life, we enter into an intimate relationship with God as daughters and sons, as beloved heirs of God's Kingdom. As we grow in our awareness of this marvelous gift of Life given us so freely, may our hearts expand ever more and more to receive what God gives.

Such a gift, this Divine Life! Such a gift, this Word made flesh! Such a gift, this message of love! But even in this graced season when we celebrate Jesus' birth into human life, we are reminded that this holy birth had its cost for Jesus—and has its cost for us. Jesus is brought to the "glory of his Resurrection" by his passion and cross. Divine Life and glory has its cost: fidelity to God's will and ways. This would not be so if we humans were not so weak, were not sinful, and were not those who stray from God's revelation of inspired word that guides us in right ways.

Jesus did not suffer and die because this was God's wish for the Divine Son. No, Jesus suffered and died because receiving his message of love and invitation into intimate relationship with his Father necessitates our giving up our human ways, our blind adherence to human laws, our clinging to our own self-righteousness at the cost of care and mercy toward others. Jesus suffered and died because of human obstinacy. His suffering and death opened a door for us to let go of these human ways that take us from God and embrace a life of love that brings us ever closer to God.

This Collect reminds us that we cannot celebrate Christmas isolated from Good Friday and Easter. The whole Mystery of Christ includes his birth into our human life and, through our participation in his suffering and death, our being raised up to share in the glory of his Divine Life. Christmas and Easter are two sides of the same coin that speak to us of salvation, of God's infinite love for us, of God's gracious gift of Life for us.

To Ponder

- I know that God has poured forth divine grace into my heart because . . . This brings me to . . .

- In order to live faithfully as Jesus has taught me, I must suffer . . . I must die to myself in these ways . . .

- The glory I experience when I give myself over to God is . . .

Prayer

Almighty God,
you have spoken to us from the beginning of creation
    through judges and kings, prophets and saints.
You have spoken the most eloquent divine word
    in the Word Made Flesh who dwells among us.
May we hear that Word,
live his Gospel,
grow in the grace you offer us,
embrace whatever suffering and dying to self may be asked of us,
and one day share in the everlasting glory of his Resurrection.
We ask this through Christ our Lord. Amen.

2.3   ARMED WITH SELF-RESTRAINT

Roman Missal Text

> Grant, O Lord, that we may begin with holy fasting
> this campaign of Christian service,
> so that, as we take up battle against spiritual evils,
> we may be armed with weapons of self-restraint.
> Through our Lord Jesus Christ, your Son,
> who lives and reigns with you in the unity of the Holy Spirit,
> one God, for ever and ever. Amen.
>
> —Collect, Ash Wednesday

Reflection

This Collect refers to Lent as a "campaign of Christian service." A campaign is organized action directed toward a particular and desirable goal. Political aspirants run an election campaign. Armies undergo a military campaign. Leaders for a cause may campaign for money and other kinds of support. During Lent, we campaign for conversion, and one way to turn one's life around is to practice Christian service. Caring for others, loving others is what Lent is all about. It is not about discipline for discipline's sake. It is about self-discipline that leads to deeper relationships, more Christ-like living, and an increase of our desire for union with God. In a real way, by growing in holiness during Lent we render our brothers and sisters in Christ a good service, for if we build up ourselves as a member of the Body of Christ, we build up the whole Body of Christ. Christian service is more than a matter of doing for others. It requires being for others.

To meet the demands of conversion and Christian service, we are invited during Lent to arm ourselves with "weapons of self-restraint." The Gospel for Ash Wednesday clearly spells out that our spiritual weapons are prayer, fasting, and works of charity (Matthew 6:1–6, 16–18). Christian penance has always had these three prongs as the visible face of its practice, and they work together to help us overcome our self-absorption and gain greater self-restraint. Each of these Lenten practices helps us grow in our relationships in a particular way. Prayer directs us more engagingly toward God. Fasting empties us of our own appetites so that we hunger for what helps us grow into the image of God in which we were created. Works of charity are ways to embrace others and give of ourselves and our material means. All of these penitential practices help us to set better priorities for our relationships by forming better habits of relating with God, self, and others.

Perhaps this overly militaristic language—campaign, battle, arm, weapons—does not appeal very much to us who are peace-loving and gentle of soul. These images do alert us to the fact that something very important is at stake not only during Lent but also during every day of our lives. We must always be attentive to whatever leads us away from holiness, whatever spiritual evils confront us. Struggling against evil is just that: a struggle. It is a battle between self-will and God's will, between satisfaction with who and where we are and the challenge to grow in holiness, between giving into temptation and resisting straying off the path of righteousness. Lent is a formal and concentrated period of time that describes our whole journey toward God. Lent is a time to form good spiritual habits and learn the kind of self-restraint that brings us fuller Life in Christ.

To Ponder

- During this Lent, the battles I must wage are . . .

- The Lenten practice that will most help me come to greater holiness during this Lent is . . .

- I am most aware that my Christian service helps me grow in my relationships with God, self, and others when . . .

Prayer

God of mercy and compassion,
you look not so much upon our sins
as upon our feeble efforts to serve you and others ever more graciously.
During this gifted time of the season of Lent,
help us to learn good habits of prayer, fasting, and works of charity
that lead to conversion of self and new Life in you.
May our battle with spiritual evil be sure and victorious,
so that we can come to Easter with hearts renewed.
We ask this through Christ our Lord. Amen.

2.4   Riches Hidden in Christ

Roman Missal Text

> Grant, almighty God,
> through the yearly observances of holy Lent,
> that we may grow in understanding
> of the riches hidden in Christ
> and by worthy conduct pursue their effects.
> Through our Lord Jesus Christ, your Son,
> who lives and reigns with you in the unity of the Holy Spirit,
> one God, for ever and ever. Amen.
>
> —Collect, First Sunday of Lent

Reflection

Most growth is a slow process. We spend a lifetime growing into being elderly and possessing wisdom and broad experience. It takes years for an acorn to grow into a mighty oak. It takes months and much trial and error for an idea to blossom into a useful invention. So it is quite understandable that our spiritual growth is also a slow process. This Collect hints at this slow spiritual growth when it speaks of "yearly observances of holy Lent." Not just one Lent will bring about the kind of conversion that leads to fullness of Life. It takes many observances. What helps us to embrace Lent with new enthusiasm for spiritual growth is the reminder that we are not the same person we were a year ago. We've had a year to grow and change. We've had a year to form better habits of good decision-making, quick forgiveness of others, more loving relationships. We don't come to this Lent the same as last year. We come having grown in our spiritual living, and so we embrace Lent with new expectations and energy.

The kind of growth we desire is pointedly spelled out in this Collect. We desire to grow in understanding of the "riches hidden in Christ." The phrase "riches hidden in Christ" calls to mind a similar phrase of St. Paul where he refers to the mystery hidden from all ages (see Colossians 1:26; also, Ephesians 3:9). Paul makes explicit that this mystery is none other than Christ himself (see Colossians 2:3 and 3:3). Our riches are Christ himself, who desires to accompany us along our journey of conversion and holiness. These riches are not hidden in the sense that children play hide-and-seek, not in the sense that they are someplace out there to be found. Rather, hidden here means concealed as in a secret. This "secret" can be known to anyone who wishes; it is not an exclusive secret. The twist here is that to know the secret we must come to know Christ, and this is part of the work of conversion during Lent. The riches God wants us to have—salvation and fullness of Life—are hidden in Christ until we encounter Christ and come to know him more deeply as our way and truth and Life.

The Collect further prays that we pursue the fruits of our Lenten observances through "worthy conduct." This way of living must be first characterized by our pursuit of Christ himself. We do this in prayer, surely, but the other two prongs of Lenten penance also bring us closer to Christ. Our fasting curbs our appetites and refocuses us on hungering for Christ and Christ alone. In fasting, we curb not only our physical appetite of hunger, but also our emotional appetites. In other words, we make a concerted effort to sort out our wants from our needs. Our works of charity help us to recognize Christ in the other person. By doing good for others we form a habit of self-giving, so much like who Christ is—the self-giving Divine Son who said yes to his Father's will and yes to our humanity. In other words, we make a concerted effort to sort out the mistaken, false riches of living for ourselves and pursue the unfathomable, true riches of the goodness of other brothers and sisters in Christ.

The "riches hidden in Christ" are even more than encountering the Divine Son, the Word made flesh who dwells within and among us. These riches include our own call to discipleship; our hearing God's inspired, revealed word; our invitation to share in Divine Life; the promise that those who are faithful to their baptismal call to die and rise with Christ will one day enjoy the fullness of Life and Christ's risen glory. The riches hidden in Christ include the privilege of being Christ's risen Presence for others, of living the Gospel and announcing it to others by the very way we live, of spending ourselves as Christ did, because by losing our Life we find it (see Matthew 16:25; Mark 8:35; Luke 2:24; John 12:25). Our life is Christ.

To Ponder

- What I can do to encounter and come to know Christ more intimately is . . .

- The "riches hidden in Christ" that I know have been given me are . . . They bring me to . . .

Prayer

Ever wise and loving God,
you reveal yourself to us through the risen Presence of your Divine Son.
Oh, how rich is that Gift to us!
Oh, how rich is all you have given us!
May we grow in our understanding of your goodness,
be strengthened to live the Gospel more perfectly
by Christ's risen presence,
and desire with all our hearts
to live worthily of the gifts you have granted us.
We ask this through Christ our Lord. Amen.

2.5 THE REALITY OF HUMAN FLESH

Roman Missal Text

O God, who willed that your Word
should take on the reality of human flesh
in the womb of the Virgin Mary,
grant, we pray,
that we, who confess our Redeemer to be God and man,
may merit to become partakers even in his divine nature.
Who lives and reigns with you in the unity of the Holy Spirit,
one God, for ever and ever. Amen.

—Collect, Solemnity of the Annunciation of the Lord

Reflection

On the Solemnity of the Annunciation of the Lord, we are reminded of just how human Jesus is. We celebrate on this day Gabriel's visit to Mary and his announcement to her that she would conceive by the Holy Spirit and become the mother of Jesus, our Savior. God did not force this exalted role on her; she freely accepted it with her yes to God. With her yes, the Son of God was incarnated—became flesh—in Mary's womb.

It took a long time for the early Church to hammer out how Jesus can be both God and human. This is a singular mystery—only Jesus is both fully God and fully human. In the course of Church history, we have been much more comfortable believing that Jesus is divine than that he is fully human. It makes more sense for us to think of Jesus primarily as divine. It is easier to turn to Jesus when we think of him primarily as divine. All his miracles, all his self-giving love, all his defeat of death, and the powers of evil point to a Divine Being. Nonetheless, the Annunciation reminds us of just how human Jesus truly is.

Mary said yes to conceiving and giving birth to Jesus. It was God's will that Jesus take on the "reality of human flesh." He didn't take on human flesh as simply a convenient masquerade so that he could work his divine powers among us. No, he truly took on the whole reality of human flesh. He became like us in everything except sin. Jesus knew pain and suffering. He experienced temptation. He showed the same emotions we do: love and sadness, tenderness and compassion, anger and frustration, care and concern, patience and courage, playfulness and determination. The reality of human flesh that Jesus took on included every possible human experience—nothing of our reality was excluded, not even death.

By identifying so completely with our human condition, Jesus could lift us above our own weakness and sinfulness, offering us the health and well-being that is salvation. Jesus was so much like us that he could draw us to himself in such a profound way that we "become partakers even in his divine nature." How we merit this share in Divine Life is by imitating Jesus' human life. We must live as he did with all the goodness and truth that he showed us.

We might say that Jesus was able to be so holy and whole because he was also divine. And this is true. Jesus' goodness and love were grounded in his Father's goodness and love, in which he shares through his divine nature. But what this Collect is telling us is that we can be holy and whole because we share in his divine nature. God gives us the gift of Divine Life, and it is this grace, this gift, this holiness, that enables us to live like Jesus. Jesus' Incarnation by the power of the Holy Spirit in the womb of the Virgin Mary is our entry into a share in his divine nature. The mystery of the Incarnation is truly the mystery of our salvation.

To Ponder

- The reality of human flesh that most enables me to live like Jesus is . . .

- The reality of human flesh that tempts me to live in another way is . . .

- Coming to a greater awareness that I partake in Jesus' divine nature means that I . . .

Prayer

Almighty God,
your Son was made flesh in the womb of Mary
and became like us in all things except sin.
Help us to live the dignity of sharing our humanity
    with your Divine Son
and being raised up to a share in his divinity.
May we live the Gospel with fidelity and truth
that we may always show by our very lives
    gratitude for your great gift of grace.
We ask this through Christ our Lord. Amen.

2.6   YOUTHFULNESS OF SPIRIT

Roman Missal Text

May your people exult for ever, O God,
in renewed youthfulness of spirit,
so that, rejoicing now in the restored glory of our adoption,
we may look forward in confident hope
to the rejoicing of the day of resurrection.
Through our Lord Jesus Christ, your Son,
who lives and reigns with you in the unity of the Holy Spirit,
one God, for ever and ever. Amen.

—Collect, Third Sunday of Easter

Reflection

From Ponce de León's search for the fountain of youth taking him to Florida in the early sixteenth century, it seems like we all are hunting for that spring of water that will keep us eternally young. So many cosmetic products advertised today are really just a masquerading of the modern search for the fountain of youth. For all our efforts, however, we all know that the aging process is inevitable. This Collect, however, does promise us a fountain of youth, and this one is sure!

As we exult in Easter joy, we are reminded that this spring festival renews our "youthfulness of spirit." This doesn't mean that we can turn back the clock on the aging process. What it does mean is that by participating in Christ's Paschal Mystery, in his self-emptying and exaltation, we already have a foot in eternity. And in eternity there is no chronological time, no aging, no duration. In eternity, we just are—totally immersed in God. During this Easter festival, when we celebrate our Lenten conversion into being more perfectly members of Christ's Body, we rejoice that God overlooks our human weaknesses and invites us into a share in divine, risen Life. As our hearts are renewed, we express a youthful energy to do God's will, a youthful enthusiasm for Life in the Holy Spirit, a youthful trust and hope in the intimate relationship into which we are invited as God receives us as adopted daughters and sons.

Life in the Holy Spirit is Life in God. It is a Life that has no limits on self-giving and generosity, happiness and holiness, joy and rejoicing. Like youth, we know that the whole responsibility for growing into mature stature as members of the Body of Christ is not entirely on our shoulders. The risen Christ is always with us through the Presence of the Holy Spirit, urging us to open ourselves to the Spirit's gifts of wisdom, understanding, counsel, fortitude, knowledge, piety, and fear of the Lord (see Isaiah 11:2–3). Blessed with these gifts, we can live the joy of the Resurrection in all we do. Every act we do—no matter how serious and consequential, or simple and unassuming—is an expression of our "youthfulness of spirit." We never tire of doing good, for this is how we express who we are in Christ and his Spirit.

No, we do not need to travel the world looking for a fountain of youth. It is here, right in our midst. We are plunged into the baptismal font and receive an eternal "youthfulness of spirit." In Christ we are ever new to the many opportunities which come our way to make visible the joy and Life of the Resurrection. We are ever young in Christ. Eternity is not aging but ageless, unbounded rejoicing in God's Life and holiness.

To Ponder

- The youthfulness I seek is . . .
- The gifts of "youthfulness of spirit" I have experienced are . . .
- Easter joy renews me through the year in that . . .

Prayer

Eternal God of love and Life,
you shower us with gifts of youthfulness and full Spirit.
May we ever grow in wisdom, understanding,
    counsel, courage, knowledge of spiritual things,
    reverence for your holy Name,
and awe for your mighty deeds of salvation.
We ask this through Christ our Lord. Amen.

2.7   LEFT US A MEMORIAL

Roman Missal Text

O God, who in this wonderful Sacrament
have left us a memorial of your Passion,
grant us, we pray,
so to revere the sacred mysteries of your Body and Blood
that we may always experience in ourselves
the fruits of your redemption.
Who live and reign with God the Father
in the unity of the Holy Spirit,
one God, for ever and ever. Amen.

—Collect, The Most Holy Bodyand Blood of Christ [Corpus Christi]

Reflection

At the Last Supper, Jesus said to those disciples gathered that they were to "Do this in remembrance of me" (Luke 22:19). The Eucharist that we celebrate is obedience to this command. Each time we celebrate the sacred mysteries we are responding to what Jesus asked of us. Surely, what we celebrate is a wonderful Sacrament. It is the continual gift of Jesus to us. The Sacrament of the Eucharist makes visible his eternal self-giving.

Eucharist is a memorial of Jesus' passion. We usually come to Eucharist with joy in our hearts, ever so grateful for his Body and Blood, which is our nourishment and strength for life. But we can never forget that it is a memorial of Jesus' passion. Jesus passed through death to give us Life. When we call it a memorial, we are saying something very specific. We are not redoing the Last Supper. We are not copying the actions and gestures that Jesus did with his disciples long ago. By responding to his command to "Do this in remembrance of me," we are participating in Jesus' continued self-giving. The very meaning of what he did at the Last Supper—giving himself over for our salvation—is made actual in our gathering and celebrating. Memorial is an active participation here and now in Jesus' act of self-giving.

If this is our active participation in Jesus' act of self-giving, then Eucharist demands something of us. We ourselves are to give ourselves over. As the bread and wine are placed on the altar, we place ourselves on the altar. As these gifts are changed in the real Body and Blood of Christ, we ourselves are transformed by the action of the Holy Spirit into being the very Body of Christ—we experience in ourselves our own identity as Body of Christ begun at our Baptism. Baptism and Eucharist can never be separated. Both are ongoing expressions of our identity with Jesus' self-giving. Participation in these sacraments is our commitment to take the fruits of our redemption given us so wondrously and generously and give them over for the good of others.

How can we not revere this wonderful Sacrament? Even as it calls us to enter into Jesus' passion with him—to pledge ourselves to dying to self, to self-emptying for the good of others—it also calls us to share in the Life of the Resurrection. Eucharist always celebrates the Resurrection because it always gives the Gift of the risen Jesus. This Gift is our Life, our salvation, our nourishment, our pledge of eternal fullness of Life. No wonder this Sacrament is called *Eucharist*, a word that means "thanksgiving." As we grow in our appreciation for Jesus' continual self-gift, our hearts cannot help but burst with love and gratitude for Jesus' true Presence, for his Body and Blood.

To Ponder

- I grasp that my participation in Eucharist also means I participate in Jesus' passion when I . . . This leads me to . . .

- I am grateful for the gift of Jesus' Body and Blood in the Eucharist for these reasons . . .

Prayer

Redeeming God,
the great joy of receiving your risen Son's Body and Blood
    in the Eucharist
is also a call to share in his passion.
Guide us in the kind of self-giving that brings Life to others.
Nourish us to be faithful to the Gospel.
Enrich us with encounters with your risen Son
so we may always have hearts filled with gratitude
    for the gifts he has won for us.
We ask this through Christ our Lord. Amen.

2.8   BECOME GOD'S DWELLING PLACE

Roman Missal Text

> O God, who teach us that you abide
> in hearts that are just and true,
> grant that we may be so fashioned by your grace
> as to become a dwelling pleasing to you.
> Through our Lord Jesus Christ, your Son,
> who lives and reigns with you in the unity of the Holy Spirit,
> one God, for ever and ever. Amen.
>
> —Collect, Sixth Sunday in Ordinary Time

Reflection

God dwells in "hearts that are just and true." What does this heart look like? A just heart is one that is in right relationship with God, self, and others. It is a righteous heart, one well founded on Gospel values that we have been taught by Jesus. A just heart is one that seeks the good of others, is not self-centered and self-serving, that cares for others as Jesus cared for all those whom he met when he walked here on earth. A true heart is one that strives always to be in accord with the Gospel. It is a heart that is in touch with reality, that does not turn from difficult choices and actions, that says yes to God with abandon and confidence. Hearts that are "just and true" are hearts aflame with the fire of God's love, with the warmth of God's compassion, with the sureness of God's own fidelity.

These kinds of hearts are ones that are not hard, but soft and pliable, open to conversion and new ways of journeying toward God. These hearts are willing to be fashioned by God's grace—that is, fashioned by God's very Life. Hearts that welcome the abiding presence of God pulse with everything God's Life is and bring joy and peace, happiness and wholesomeness, fullness and faithfulness. The pulse of these hearts is not only in tune with God and God's ways, but is also in tune with others and their joys and sorrows, needs and concerns, struggles and pain. To have hearts fashioned by God's grace means that God's commandments are not a burden, but an opportunity to express our own fidelity to God's ways. God's gifts are never wasted on anything less than that which brings health and well-being (that is, salvation) to self and others. God's Presence is received with life-changing exuberance.

How awesome to think that just and true hearts are pleasing to our God! Each one of us makes a difference to God! Our God—Creator, Redeemer, Sanctifier—chooses to make of us a divine dwelling place. This is our dignity as those created in God's very image. Full hearts demand that we are eager to protect this divine indwelling. When God's Presence within is constantly before our hearts and eyes, it is so much easier to choose to do God's will, to choose to do the holy thing, to choose to be Life-givers as God is. All of this good is God's work. All we need do is open our hearts in surrender to God's grace, and welcome God's abiding Presence.

To Ponder

- For my heart to be more just and true, I must . . .

- I am fully aware of pleasing God when I . . .

Prayer

Amazing God,
you are pleased to make your divine dwelling within us.
Help us become ever more aware of your Presence
and to act only in ways that please you.
Fill us with the hope and desire
that one day we will dwell forever with you in fullness of Life.
We ask this through Christ our Lord. Amen.

2.9   IN THE COURSE OF OUR WORLD

Roman Missal Text

> Grant us, O Lord, we pray,
> that the course of our world
> may be directed by your peaceful rule
> and that your Church may rejoice,
> untroubled in her devotion.
> Through our Lord Jesus Christ, your Son,
> who lives and reigns with you in the unity of the Holy Spirit,
> one God, for ever and ever. Amen.
>
> —Collect, Eighth Sunday in Ordinary Time

Reflection

Lately, it seems that "the course of our world" is directed by anything but God's peaceful rule. The peace we lack is not simply caused by wars and insurrection, but also by genocide and senseless other kinds of killing, by greed and consumerism, by sexism and hedonism, and by just about every other "ism" under the sun. The "course of our world" certainly seems off course! We have ravaged our natural resources and have not shared them equally, have polluted our planet beyond imagination, have become so busy that we have no time to stop and smell the roses, and are inundated with every noise during every moment of every day. Finding some oasis of peace in all of this is a challenge. Nevertheless, this challenge is not beyond those of us who rejoice in God's Presence and care.

The marks of God's peaceful rule are clear enough. They are the traces of the Holy Spirit's Presence and power. These include love, joy, peace, patience, kindness, generosity, faithfulness, gentleness, and self-control (see Galatians 5:22–23). Notice how each of these is an antidote for the many ways that bring about a lack of peace. So to cooperate with God in setting the course of the world to be directed by God's peaceful rule, we must open ourselves to the prompting of the Holy Spirit and surrender ourselves to God's ways.

God's peaceful rule is not oppressive, does not seek to dominate, and cares for all with equal dignity and respect. God's peaceful rule is brought about when our relationships with each other bear the marks of the fruit of the Holy Spirit. It might seem a daunting task to look out over the horizon of our world's lack of peace and the myriads of needs, and think that we can make a difference. In this case, thinking too broadly can stifle us and keep us from action. Rather, we have to focus on our own lives, our own families and neighbors and coworkers. If we change for the better even one relationship in one of these spheres, then the world is a better place. Then God's peaceful rule is established someplace, even if it seems to be such a tiny place.

We rejoice now in all the little ways that we help peace to triumph over strife, goodness to overcome evil, health and wholeness to overcome brokenness and despair. As Church our rejoicing is full-throated, for we know that whatever healing we can bring to our world, we do so because Christ's victory over death has already redeemed our world. We are troubled when we listen to the nightly news or go to an internet news site or read a newspaper. It seems as though this wrong world-course is so far astray that we can never bring our earthly home back to God's peaceful rule. And by ourselves we cannot. But as Church, we are as strong as the Presence of the risen Christ and the indwelling of the Holy Spirit. We are given the gift of rejoicing when we turn our devotion toward God by means of our own surrender of life into God's caring hands. Only through surrender of ourselves can we be untroubled in our relationship with God and each other.

Our prayer for peace must be fervent. Our self-giving surrender must be bold. Our loving relationships must be unbreakable. Our desire for just living must be emphatic. Our concern for creation must be all-embracing. When we live in this way, "the course of our world"—at least our own little corner of the world—turns secure in God's peaceful rule.

To Ponder

- What concerns me most about my world is . . . What concerns me most about my relationships is . . .

- I am untroubled in my devotion to God when . . . This brings me to rejoice because . . .

Prayer

Almighty God,
you rule the world with justice and righteousness
and desire that we live in peace.
May all contentions cease.
May we be your instruments of lasting peace.
And until such a day
    when your peace truly reigns in all the universe,
may we hope in your victory and rejoice in your saving power.
We ask this through Christ our Lord. Amen.

2.10 GOD'S PROVIDENCE

Roman Missal Text

> O God, whose providence never fails in its design,
> keep from us, we humbly beseech you,
> all that might harm us
> and grant all that works for our good.
> Through our Lord Jesus Christ, your Son,
> who lives and reigns with you in the unity of the Holy Spirit,
> one God, for ever and ever. Amen.
>
> —Collect, Ninth Sunday in Ordinary Time

Reflection

We sometimes hear expressions like "The devil made me do it" or "It's fate." In the first expression, we are ducking our own responsibility for our choices; in the second, we are saying that everything is preordained and nothing we can do will change what will happen. Both of these expressions point to the problems of evil and freedom, which have been the content of countless theological discussions throughout the ages. The problems of evil and freedom are often connected to divine providence. Some people think that God directs absolutely everything that happens. Even when bad things happen—sickness, suffering, and death; hurricanes, tornadoes, and earthquakes—it is God's will that these things take place. Yet everything we know about our God is that God is One who loves and cares for us, whose plan is that we enjoy blessings and happiness, who desires that we come to the fullness of Life. This doesn't sound like a God who would will for us evil and disasters!

Literally, the word *providence* comes from two Latin words and means "to see before," "to have foresight." Surely God has foresight about everything that is and that happens. This is because in God there is no time as we experience it. There is no clock time; no duration of events; no past, present, or future. In God, there is only eternal now, eternal knowing of all things. God's knowing something does not make it happen. If God ordered all things, there would be no evil in the world, but neither would there be freedom. God does not want of us a forced faithfulness, an automatic response. What God wants of us is that we freely return our love for divine love, blessing for divine blessing, and human compassion for divine compassion.

God's "providence never fails in its design." This does not mean that God determines everything; that would remove the free will with which God created us. What it does mean is that the design of God's providence is that all should be ordered to good. For us, this means that God's design is that we should all come to eternal Life. But because this is God's design, God's will, it does not mean that it must be so. We are free to respond faithfully to God or not.

We pray that God "keep from us all that might harm us." We know we are weak; we know we sin; we know we stray from the path of goodness that God has set us upon from the very moment of our conception. Therefore, our prayer is one for God's guidance, protective care, and sure truth. We must often beg God to keep us from straying, to keep us on the right path toward fullness of Life. And when we do stray (and we will!), God is there to forgive us when we turn back to him.

God's providence is more even than protecting us from all that might harm us. God's protection includes giving us "all that works for our good." God gives us every strength, wisdom, insight, courage, and hope to face the challenges and temptations that come our way and helps us freely choose to do what we know God would will for us. This Collect is a very comforting one. It reminds us that God's providence is not a matter of sorting out those saved from those condemned, but rather of giving us everything we need to choose to remain faithful to God's will. This fidelity lines us up with the eternal design of God's plan for humanity and even for all creation. God's "providence never fails in its design." Even when some put themselves before God and God's ways, some others will be faithful and bring God's plan of salvation to fruition. God's faithful are God's beloved daughters and sons who steadfastly journey toward the fullness of Life God desires for each of us.

To Ponder

- I think about God's divine providence when . . . I ought to think about it when . . .

- I am most able to choose the right path to fullness of Life when I . . . I tend to stray from this path when I . . .

Prayer

Providential God,
you desire that all people come to the fullness of Life
    you have prepared for us from all eternity.
May our prayer to be faithful to your plan be fervent,
our courage to stay the course toward fidelity be strong,
and our wisdom to discern your will for us
    be a light leading us to all that you want for us.
We ask this through Christ our Lord. Amen.

2.11 THE FIRM FOUNDATION OF GOD'S LOVE

Roman Missal Text

Grant, O Lord,
that we may always revere and love your holy name,
for you never deprive of your guidance
those you set firm on the foundation of your love.
Through our Lord Jesus Christ, your Son,
who lives and reigns with you in the unity of the Holy Spirit,
one God, for ever and ever. Amen.

—Collect, Twelfth Sunday in Ordinary Time

Reflection

In biblical times, one's name identified the person in relation to a place, family of origin or clan, or something about the person, perhaps a life task. To know someone's name was to know the person. The expression "How are you?" originated in a similar way. It had nothing to do with inquiring about how the person is feeling—good or bad, sick or well—but rather how the person came about, in other words, it was an inquiry about one's lineage. One's lineage determined who someone was, the respect someone was owed, and one's place in society.

When we pray to "revere and love [God's] holy name," it is not simply a matter of not taking God's name in vain, but primarily of revering and loving God. God's name stands for God. To know God's name is to know God, and of course we cannot ever know God completely. This is why when Moses asked God's name (see Exodus 3:13), God didn't answer with very much clarity (scholars are still discussing the meaning of YHWH). God couldn't reveal the divine name because Moses couldn't know God.

Yet, through the Incarnation of Jesus, we do come to know God. Jesus promised us that if we know him, we also know his Father (see John 14:7). He who sees Jesus, sees the Father (see John 14:9). The historical Jesus is no longer among us—he has risen and taken his rightful place with God. Nevertheless, we do see Jesus in one another, for through the Holy Spirit the risen Jesus is present within and among us. By our Baptism, our own name becomes Body of Christ. If we are to "revere and love God's holy name," then we must revere and love one another. This love, however, is not merely a human love (as good as that may be), but it is a divine love. Jesus said at the Last Supper, "This is my commandment, that you love one another as I have loved you" (John 15:12). To love as Jesus did is a tall order, indeed!

God guides us in a way of living that fulfills Jesus' commandment of love. We are able to live the Gospel because God has "set us firm on the foundation of God's love." Thus it is with God's love that we love; it is by loving as Jesus did that we "revere and love God's holy name." The foundation of God's love is not a self-serving love, but a reaching out to others with the very goodness of God. God's love is goodness and self-giving made visible. This love was made visible in the goodness and self-giving of Jesus as he lived here among us, teaching us how to live, and showing us how to "revere and love God's holy name." Now, after the Resurrection and Ascension, we are the risen Christ's Presence for each other. Our love makes visible the Divine Son's love. Our love is the Divine Son's love.

This is a firm foundation upon which to build our life because this kind of loving is Gospel loving. This kind of self-giving is who Jesus was and how Jesus taught us to be—like him. This kind of love enables us to be faithful to our identity as Body of Christ, to be faithful to being named Christian, followers of Jesus. Our very being reverences and loves God when we act as the Divine Son taught us. When we love as he did.

To Ponder

- I revere and love God's holy name in these ways . . .
- My love is like Jesus' love when I . . .

Prayer

Loving God,
you have been good to us beyond what we can imagine.
We revere and love your holy name
    for you are deserving of all our adoration.
Help us to set our daily living firmly on the foundation of your love,
caring for others as you care for us.
We ask this through Christ our Lord. Amen.

2.12 THE GOOD THINGS THAT ENDURE

Roman Missal Text

> O God, protector of those who hope in you,
> without whom nothing has firm foundation, nothing is holy,
> bestow in abundance your mercy upon us
> and grant that, with you as our ruler and guide,
> we may use the good things that pass
> in such a way as to hold fast even now
> to those that ever endure.
> Through our Lord Jesus Christ, your Son,
> who lives and reigns with you in the unity of the Holy Spirit,
> one God, for ever and ever. Amen.
>
> —Collect, Seventeenth Sunday in Ordinary Time

Reflection

Alexander Pope wrote, "Hope springs eternal in the human breast." He was so very optimistic! We don't hope for bad things—we never hope to have cancer or die in a car accident or be destitute in our retirement. We always hope for, expect, and desire good things in life. We hope for a good job to take care of our family, for good health to see our children and grandchildren grow up, for steady friends who remain near us in joys and sorrows. Ultimately, we hope for an eternity of fullness of Life in God. Is this too much for which to hope?

This Collect mentions five consequences of hoping in God: God is our protector, our firm foundation, the One who is holy and in whose holiness we share, the One who bestows in abundance divine mercy, and the One who rules and guides us kindly so that our hope is increased. Everything about God's relationship with us is directed to our eternal salvation. Our hope joins us with God's benevolence.

One of the beautiful things about this Collect is that it does not condemn the things of this world, the things of God's creation. All this will pass. In the meantime, we use the good things that pass to fuel our hope, to direct us toward God's ways, to ease our trials and sufferings so that we are more free to keep our eyes on God and what God wills for us. The good things that we use are to help us "hold fast even now to those that ever endure." What endures are not the things of this world, of this creation. What endures are the things that give us hope, the things of God: mercy, love, forgiveness, holiness, goodness, and wisdom are things that last. These are all things of God. The things of creation and each other are the means by which we are able to make visible all the things of God that endure. This is especially true of the virtues that increase our right relationships with each other, for when things are right among us, things are right with God.

If our hope is to be sure, then we need to hold fast to God's gifts. "Hope springs eternal in the human breast" when we hold fast even now to those things that ever endure. We use the good things that pass, but we must come to understand that these things in themselves can never lead us to what endures. Only God endures for eternity. Our hope lies in the firm foundation of the One eternal Being in whom we find our life. We dare to ask God for an abundance of what endures. God gives. We only need be open to the divine gifts.

To Ponder

- The good things of this creation that bring me in right relationship with God and others are . . .

- My hope lies in . . . It springs eternally when . . .

Prayer

O God,
you shower your own goodness and holiness on those of us
    who use the good things of this earth
    to lead us to those things that endure.
May we ever keep our gaze on you and your divine love,
    open ourselves to your abundant mercy,
and seek only you as our firm foundation of holiness and goodness.
As we journey toward the fullness of Life you desire for us,
help us to reach out to others
with the same graciousness with which you care for us.
We ask this through Christ our Lord. Amen.

2.13 HEARTS FIXED ON TRUE GLADNESS

Roman Missal Text

O God, who cause the minds of the faithful
to unite in a single purpose,
grant your people to love what you command
and to desire what you promise,
that, amid the uncertainties of this world,
our hearts may be fixed on that place
where true gladness is found.
Through our Lord Jesus Christ, your Son,
who lives and reigns with you in the unity of the Holy Spirit,
one God, for ever and ever. Amen.

—Collect, Twenty-First Sunday in Ordinary Time

Reflection

All of us seek happiness. We are most loving, most productive, and most effective when we are happy, when we have a sense of well-being and that all is right with the world. So it is no surprise that our prayer often is directed to what we perceive to be necessary for us to be happy. But sometimes when we think like Jesus and not like ourselves, what we seek by way of happiness might surprise us.

We pray in this Collect for all of us "to unite in a single purpose." That seems like an impossible prayer! We all seek different things from life. What is happiness for one may not be so for another. Some are happy with fewer things; some need many things around them. Some are happy only when they are busy every minute; others are happy just to sit quietly and contemplate the beauty of creation and people around them. Some are happy when their own plans are being fulfilled; others are most happy when they are doing good for others. These kinds of things will hardly "unite in a single purpose." But the Collect does give us a hint of what will: we are to fix our hearts "on that place where true gladness is found." Many of us might immediately jump to thinking about heaven—surely we can be united in a single purpose about everyone meriting fullness of Life. And, yes, being with God for all eternity is surely the ultimate happiness; it is true gladness. But this doesn't mean that we cannot be truly happy here, and all united in a single purpose to merit that happiness.

True and lasting happiness is found in loving what God commands and desiring what God promises. God commands that we be faithful to what the Divine Son taught us. We are to live our baptismal covenant with God, which not only means we keep God's commandments, but also that we keep ourselves focused on God's way as the only true path to salvation. The commandments are minimal. Living with God's love, mercy, compassion, care, and generosity is far more demanding than keeping any commandment. When we align our own desires with God's desire for our salvation, then all these self-giving actions are much easier to embrace. Our true gladness is found in growing in our relationship with God and others so that our hearts are turned toward them.

When we live what God commands and desire what God promises, then the uncertainties of this world cannot shake us from our journey toward salvation and eternal happiness. We will still face many uncertainties, to be sure. God does not guarantee us a steady job with good pay, children that never stray from family values, friends who never turn their back on us. What God does guarantee is that we have everything we need to keep focused on what God promises to those who are faithful: eternal happiness, eternal Life.

To Ponder

- God promises me . . . I am willing to go to these lengths to obtain this promise . . .

- The uncertainties that I face in my life are . . . I am most aware of God's help when I . . .

Prayer

Faithful God,
you promise true gladness and happiness with you for all eternity
to those who are faithful to your commandments
and the Gospel way of living.
Unite us in this single purpose of being faithful servants,
conform our hearts to the Sacred Heart of your Divine Son,
and bring us to the fullness of Life.
We ask this through Christ our Lord. Amen.

2.14 THE GREATEST POWER

Roman Missal Text

> O God, who manifest your almighty power
> above all by pardoning and showing mercy,
> bestow, we pray, your grace abundantly upon us
> and make those hastening to attain your promises
> heirs to the treasures of heaven.
> Through our Lord Jesus Christ, your Son,
> who lives and reigns with you in the unity of the Holy Spirit,
> one God, for ever and ever. Amen.
>
> —Collect, Twenty-Sixth Sunday in Ordinary Time

Reflection

Bullying is on people's minds these days. Sad, sad stories of its consequences are all too frequently reported on the news. Bullies need power over others and pick easy prey—those whom they perceive are small, weak, vulnerable. Often this need to exercise power over another is a subconscious way to fill a void in themselves. Too often bullies are those who are abused or have been bullied themselves. This Collect speaks of power too—God's almighty power. So is God the great bully in the sky? Hardly! God's almighty power is never a power *over*, but a power *to*. God's exercise of power builds us up as the Body of Christ and enables us to journey more steadily and surely to becoming "heirs to the treasures of heaven."

We pray that God manifest "almighty power above all by pardoning and showing mercy." Now this is quite startling! We would think that the greatest manifestation of God's almighty power would be, for example, in the divine act of creation. God begins with nothing but "a formless void" (Genesis 1:2) and brings forth unimaginable variety of life in plants and animals. But most of all, God brings forth us human beings who are made in the very image and likeness of our Creator (see Genesis 1:27). Here is surely great power! Or we might think of the greatest manifestation of God's almighty power when we experience the ferocity of a storm or the rhythm and order of the vast universe. Here is surely great power! Further still, we might think of the greatest manifestation of God's almighty power when we see the delicacy of a butterfly or the quickness of a hummingbird. Here is surely great power! Yes, all this is an encounter with God's great power.

This Collect, however, sets all this wonder aside and shows us another way. In it, we pray that the greatest act of God's almighty power is manifested in the simple ways of forgiveness and mercy. There is almighty power in forgiving another! Why is it we are so slow to forgive, when this act is such a divine, power-laden act? There is almighty power in showing mercy toward another! Why is it we are so slow to show mercy? Our hesitation in acting like God indicates how far we still need to grow in our holiness. Withholding forgiveness and mercy are selfish acts, not at all God-like. When we act thus, we are placing ourselves before all others. When we embrace self-emptying, we are able, with God's grace "abundantly poured upon us," to manifest the same great power. This power is a power to renew weakened or broken relationships. What God desires most from us is wholesome and holy relationships.

We hasten to receive the "treasures in heaven" when we act as God does and offer others forgiveness and mercy. The treasure to which we are heirs is everlasting life in God. With this fullness of Life, we will have come to the wholesome and holy relationships that are Life-giving and that unite us into one Body forever in the glory of the risen Christ. Such small acts—forgiving and showing mercy—to gain so much Life!

To Ponder

- I have experienced the great power of forgiveness and mercy in these ways . . .

- The treasures to which I cling in this life are . . . The treasure I hope to obtain is . . .

Prayer

Forgiving and merciful God,
your almighty power heals all ills
and your grace binds us into one Body
who seeks to praise and give thanks to you in all things.
Help us to be more forgiving and merciful
so that our relationships with others might be strong and Life-giving.
Help us to seek forgiveness quickly when we have wronged another.
Fill our hearts with joy
that one day we will be heirs to the great treasure of heaven.
We ask this through Christ our Lord. Amen.

2.15   HASTEN WITHOUT STUMBLING

Roman Missal Text

> Almighty and merciful God,
> by whose gift your faithful offer you
> right and praiseworthy service,
> grant, we pray,
> that we may hasten without stumbling
> to receive the things you have promised.
> Through our Lord Jesus Christ, your Son,
> who lives and reigns with you in the unity of the Holy Spirit,
> one God, for ever and ever. Amen.

—Collect, Thirty-First Sunday in Ordinary Time

Reflection

It is so adorable to watch babies learn to walk. They take a few steps and get started, and then they go fast and faster until eventually they fall over. Then they get up and try again. We are all familiar with the saying "Haste makes waste." When we do something too quickly we are prone to make mistakes, to be less thorough, to take shortcuts that might come back to haunt us. This is our human experience. This Collect alerts us to divine experience, where we are so eager to merit what God has promised us that we can "hasten without stumbling." When it comes to seeking God's ways and what God has promised us, no haste can be too hasty. God is with us, journeying with us, keeping us from stumbling. Our haste is an expression of our own expectation and eagerness.

Everything we are and have is a gift from God. This Collect does not specify the gift (no doubt God's grace), but rather the effects of our receiving God's gift. First, we can offer God "right and praiseworthy service." Before we jump too quickly to what we do in service for others, we must step back and consider that our primary service is to God. We fulfill this service when we participate in Mass and the other sacraments. We fulfill this service when we are faithful to daily prayer, forming a habit of keeping God foremost in our thoughts and daily living. We fulfill this service when we take time to contemplate the many ways God's Presence is manifested to us and offer hearts filled with gratitude. All of these are "right and praiseworthy acts of service" that we give the God whose grace it is that even enables us to perform this service. Without God, we can do nothing.

When we are faithful to this kind of "right and praiseworthy service," our daily actions overflow in easy and graceful service of others. We not only "hasten without stumbling" to receive the promise of fullness of Life from God, but with God as the center of our lives we also hasten without stumbling to do good for others. If there is any hurrying in our lives, it ought to be for the sake of others. If there is any hurrying in our lives, it ought to be manifesting the care and concern that eases the burdens of others. Ironically, by easing the burden of others our own yoke becomes lighter and easier to carry (see Matthew 11:30).

It is important to note that this Collect appears near the end of the liturgical year. The Collects upon which we've been meditating from preceding Sundays, and others used at this time of year, speak strongly about God's promise of fullness of Life. We are moving toward the Solemnity of Our Lord Jesus Christ, King of the Universe, which ends the liturgical year. We celebrate Christ's victory over sin and death and our own participation in the salvation he has won for us. As we look forward to Christ's Second Coming at the end of time, we anticipate with great joy that day when we will share fully in the same risen Life and glory he has. This is certainly a good thing to have on our minds!

To Ponder

- The right and praiseworthy service I offer to God and others is . . .

- I hasten without stumbling to . . . What I have already received is . . .

Prayer

Glorious God,
you promise us every good thing
and give us all we need to merit receiving what you have promised.
Grace us with your continued Presence
that we may never stumble in our journey toward you
and the promise of fullness of Life.
We ask this through Christ our Lord. Amen.

CHAPTER 3

TEXTS DRAWN FROM THE PREFACES

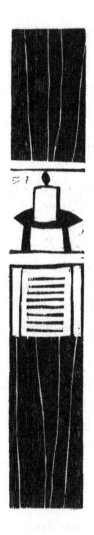

In English, the word *preface* refers to part of the front matter of a book, often giving the reason for the author's writing the book, interest in the subject, or acknowledgment of those who encouraged the work. So we can easily misconstrue this word in such a way that we think of the Preface at Mass as something coming before the Eucharistic Prayer and apart from it. But it is actually the first part of the Eucharistic Prayer. The Preface of the Eucharistic Prayer might say something about the feast or season, retell some of God's marvelous deeds on our behalf, recount for us God's love in creation and salvation.

Some of our Eucharistic Prayers have their own Prefaces. For the most part, though, the Preface changes according to the season or festival. They are rich in theological content and set the tone for how we hear the rest of the Eucharistic Prayer.

3.1   LIFT UP YOUR HEARTS

Roman Missal Text

> The Lord be with you. And with your Spirit.
> Lift up your hearts. We lift them up to the Lord.
> Let us give thanks to the Lord our God. It is right and just.

—no. 31

Reflection

Called the "Preface Dialogue," these three short versicles and responses not only begin the Preface, but the entire Eucharistic Prayer. Delving into what we are saying can lead us deeper into the whole prayer. This exchange between priest and assembly is very old, dating to the very earliest times. It is one of the most invariable parts of the entire Mass. No matter what Preface or Eucharistic Prayer we choose, this dialogue always begins the Eucharistic Prayer. We have already reflected on the first of the exchanges in part 1 of this book,[7] so in this meditation we focus on the second and third dialogues.

For all of our care in this new translation, and for all of the changes, the middle dialogue is exactly what we've been saying in English in the past decades. This is unfortunate, because a more literal translation of the Latin phrases opens up a richer meaning. Some of us are old enough to remember the Latin: *Sursum corda. Habemus ad Dominum.* There is no explicit verb in either Latin phrase, which works well in Latin, but poses some problems for the English translation. *Sursum* means "upward" or "on high" and *corda* means "hearts." So, a more literal translation of *sursum corda* would be "upward hearts" or "hearts on high." The people's response is more literally translated, "we have them to the Lord." This exchange suggests that our hearts are already with the Lord. It suggests a readiness for prayer, because our hearts are where they are supposed to be. Union with God and readiness is our whole "posture" during the Eucharistic Prayer. The priest gestures for the whole community—his hands are extended in an *orans* position—that is, his outstretched arms and palms lift our prayers and ourselves upward toward God. While we all know that heaven is not a physical space, the imagery here hints that we have joined the heavenly choir in order to give God thanks and praise. We have totally turned toward God and desire to be one heart with God.

This reflection sets up a richer meaning for the last of the three Preface Dialogues. We are invited to "give thanks to the Lord our God." Our thanks well up from hearts that are already in communion with the Divine Presence. A typical Preface enumerates some of God's mighty deeds on our behalf and for our

---

7. See 1.5.

salvation. Our thankful hearts anticipate God's continuing actions on our behalf, especially in what takes place in the Eucharistic Prayer. We answer this invitation to gratitude with "It is right and just." These words are repeated in the opening line of the Preface Prayer. Yes, it belongs to our very *dignity* (the Latin is *dignum*) as those created in God's image and likeness and redeemed by the Blood of the Lamb that we give thanks to almighty God. Being thus created and redeemed, through our Baptism we are privileged to be in an intimate relationship with God. The word *just* here (the Latin is *iustum*) points to a relationship. Even our thanksgiving shows a boldness on our part in addressing our God and reveling in the Divine Presence, a gift of intimate relationship merited only by our heartfelt thanksgiving and praise, by our *sursum corda*.

To Ponder

- I not only give God thanks at Mass, but I always give thanks for . . .
- I would describe my relationship with God as . . .
- What helps me grow in this relationship is . . .

Prayer

Our hearts are turned toward you, Lord God almighty,
    in gratitude and praise for all the good you have done for us.
You have created us,
your Son has redeemed us,
your Spirit has sanctified us in your Life and holiness.
Help us to live faithfully the dignity you have bestowed upon us
    as your beloved daughters and sons,
an unequaled and intimate relationship.
Help us to raise our hearts to you in gratitude in all things
and in every way.
We ask this through Christ our Lord. Amen.

3.2   STRETCHED OUT HIS HANDS

Roman Missal Text

> It is truly right and just, our duty and our salvation,
> always and everywhere to give you thanks, Father most holy,
> through your beloved Son, Jesus Christ,
> your Word through whom you made all things,
> whom you sent as our Savior and Redeemer,
> incarnate by the Holy Spirit and born of the Virgin.
> Fulfilling your will and gaining for you a holy people,
> he stretched out his hands as he endured his Passion,
> so as to break the bonds of death and manifest the resurrection.
> And so, with the Angels and all the Saints
> we declare your glory,
> as with one voice we acclaim:
>
> —Preface, Eucharistic Prayer II, no. 99

Reflection

Eucharistic Prayer II is used so often, with its own Preface, that we might easily fall into the habit of simply not listening to its words. This Preface follows classical lines, mentioning creation, the Incarnation, salvation, and our holiness in Christ. It is well that we take some time to reflect on this prayer.

The Preface calls Jesus the Word who was present at creation. This echoes the beginning of the Gospel of John: "In the beginning was the Word and the Word was with God and the Word was God. . . . All things came into being through him. . . . " (John 1:1, 3). In Hebrew, "word" is *dabar*, which can have many meanings. When applied to God as in "God's word," it is always an active, powerful, productive, fruitful word. When God speaks, something happens. Thus at creation "God said . . . ," and the world and we ourselves came into being. The most eloquent and fruitful word God speaks is the Word made flesh, the Divine Son. Coexistent with God, the Word was "incarnate by the Holy Spirit." This Divine Word took on flesh and blood, became one with us in all things but sin. This almighty Word spoken by God is "our Savior and Redeemer."

Salvation and redemption came about because this Word was totally obedient to God's will and in this obedience showed us how we are to live. We are a holy people when we do as Jesus did: he "stretched out his hands" on the cross. These nailed and outstretched hands not only endured the Passion, but also embrace each of us in Jesus' saving act of breaking "the bonds of death" and bringing us to the new Life of the Resurrection. Holiness is of God; when we surrender ourselves to Jesus' saving embrace, we ourselves share in Divine Life, we ourselves become of God, we ourselves are holy.

What is asked of us in this Preface is surrender to the risen Christ's embrace of all of us. This surrender is how we ourselves are obedient to God's will. And in turn each of us must assume the posture of Jesus on the cross: stretch out our own hands to embrace all those whom we encounter in our daily living. Like Jesus we want to invite everyone into obedience to God's will, embrace everyone with our own love and care, and help bring others to the fullness of Life that God offers us in the risen Christ.

To Ponder

- As Jesus stretched out his hands, I stretch out my hands when I . . . My embrace includes . . .

- Surrendering myself to God's will is an experience of obedience when I . . . It is an experience of holiness when I . . .

Prayer

Holy God,
you invite us into a share of your Divine Life
when we are obedient to your holy will as was your Divine Son.
Help us to listen for what you ask of us,
to accept your will for our life and holiness,
and to stretch out our own hands to embrace others
and lead them into your loving arms.
We ask this through Christ our Lord. Amen.

3.3 LOVE SO TIGHT

Roman Missal Text

> It is truly right and just
> that we should always give you thanks,
> Lord, holy Father, almighty and eternal God.
> For you do not cease to spur us on
> to possess a more abundant life
> and, being rich in mercy,
> you constantly offer pardon
> and call on sinners
> to trust in your forgiveness alone.
> Never did you turn away from us,
> and, though time and again we have broken your covenant,
> you have bound the human family to yourself
> through Jesus your Son, our Redeemer,
> with a new bond of love so tight
> that it can never be undone.
> Even now you set before your people
> a time of grace and reconciliation,
> and, as they turn back to you in spirit,
> you grant them hope in Christ Jesus
> and a desire to be of service to all,
> while they entrust themselves
> more fully to the Holy Spirit.
> And so, filled with wonder,
> we extol the power of your love,
> and, proclaiming our joy
> at the salvation that comes from you,
> we join in the heavenly hymn of countless hosts,
> as without end we acclaim:
>
> —Preface, Eucharistic Prayer for Reconciliation I, 1

Reflection

How consoling is this Preface! God never "ceases to spur us on" toward a fuller and richer Life. Even when through our own willfulness and weakness we sin—we turn our backs on God—God still urges us to seek God's greatest gift: "a more abundant life." God is the God of Life and is most gracious and patient in coaxing us into this Life. God "spurs us on" because God is a God of mercy and compassion. Even when we turn away from God, God never turns away from us. Instead of turning away from us, God binds us with "love so tight" that we have to fight to break away from God. We do not accidentally fall into sin—we work at sinning, at pushing ourselves away from God's "love so tight."

How consoling is this Preface! God sets before God's "people a time of grace and reconciliation." The Eucharist is the Sacrament of Reconciliation par excellence. This, because in the Eucharist God invites us into a covenantal intimacy with him and with each other. In Eucharist, we are invited to be one with the Divine Son and partake at his banquet of love and abundance. It is no ordinary food that satisfies us at this banquet. Our food at this banquet is the very Body and Blood of our Lord Jesus Christ. By partaking of this food, we become more perfectly who we are—the Body of Christ. Eucharist is a sacrament of reconciliation because it is a sacrament of unity. We cannot be one in the Body of Christ at the same time we exclude others, hold grudges, and harbor broken relationships. The Eucharist calls us to let go of what divides and embrace what reconciles us to God and each other.

What reconciles is the "bond of" love so tight "that it can never be undone." This kind of love originates in God, is God. This kind of love helps us let go of all our own pettiness and embrace God's way of mercy and compassion, forgiveness and unity. This kind of love is much stronger than the selfishness that separates. It is the love so tight that we never want to remove ourselves from it. It is a love that is God's very Life.

To Ponder

- I find myself straying from God and others most often when I . . .

- The "love so tight" that brings me to reconciliation is . . .

- God's great love moves me to . . . My love moves me to . . . My love moves others to . . .

Prayer

God of love,
your Life draws us into the bond of perfect love with you,
a love so tight that it can never be broken.
Open us to this goodness and Life;
help us to seek unity in all things rather than divisions,
and to be merciful and forgiving of others as you are toward us.
We ask this through Christ our Lord. Amen.

3.4 LONGING FOR CHRIST

Roman Missal Text

> It is truly right and just, our duty and our salvation,
> always and everywhere to give you thanks,
> Lord, holy Father, almighty and eternal God,
> through Christ our Lord.
> For all the oracles of the prophets foretold him,
> the Virgin Mother longed for him
> with love beyond all telling,
> John the Baptist sang of his coming
> and proclaimed his presence when he came.
> It is by his gift that already we rejoice
> at the mystery of his Nativity,
> so that he may find us watchful in prayer
> and exultant in his praise.
> And so, with Angels and Archangels,
> with Thrones and Dominions,
> and with all the hosts and Powers of heaven,
> we sing the hymn of your glory,
> as without end we acclaim:
>
> —Preface II of Advent, no. 34

Reflection

The "prophets foretold" the coming of the Messiah. However, like so many things, we only hear what we want to hear. We hear the prophets foretell the coming of a king (see, for example, Isaiah 9:1–7) as well as a suffering servant (see Isaiah 42:1–4; 49:1–6; 50:4–9; 52:13—53:12). But who wants to hear about suffering? What was foremost in the minds of those looking for the coming of a Messiah was that he would be a powerful king who would restore Israel to a nation with wealth, vast lands, and respect from all. No wonder so many missed the coming of the Messiah. He came as a King, to be sure, but not according to their expectations. He came as a Servant-King, one who would suffer for the infidelities of God's holy people.

Mary, too, lives in expectation of the Messiah; in the Preface, we pray that the "Virgin Mother longed for him with love beyond all telling." We so focus on the divine miracle of the Incarnation—the Son of God taking on human flesh—that we sometimes miss the human drama that unfolded among those who were God's instruments. Do we think about Mary being pregnant for nine months, wondering all that time about the child to be born who was not conceived in the ordinary human way? Do we think about Mary longing for the birth, anticipating the joy of new life coming into the world? Do we think about Mary, almost due, riding that donkey so many miles from Nazareth to Bethlehem? No doubt Mary longed for this birth like every pregnant mother longs for a healthy baby. Oh, how her longing was fulfilled!

Advent calls us to wait and wonder, expect and anticipate, long for and savor the coming of the Servant-King-Messiah. The mystery of the Nativity is as much about longing as it is about birthing. For even now, we long for the coming of the Messiah—daily in our prayer and faithful servant-works. Like Mary, we must be "watchful in prayer and exultant in praise." This is a time to have great longing for the triumph, but also for the necessary self-emptying, that marks those who are striving to live as this Servant-King-Messiah taught us. Our longing must be as long as Mary's, as Life-giving as Mary's, and as joyful and praise-filled as Mary's. Advent is Mary's season to teach us how to keep the Divine Son within and near all the days of our lives.

To Ponder

- I long for Jesus to come to me with "love beyond all telling" when I . . .

- I experience both the joy and the suffering of the mystery of the Incarnation in these ways . . .

Prayer

God of the prophets,
of John the Baptist,
of Mary,
and of each of us,
we long to open ourselves to your Divine Presence
and to love beyond all telling
as Jesus has taught us.
Open our hearts to the gift of his love
and help us to hear the Gospel with new ears
and new resolve to empty ourselves for the good of others.
We ask this through Christ our Lord. Amen.

3.5   THIS AWE-FILLED MYSTERY

Roman Missal Text

It is truly right and just, our duty and our salvation,
always and everywhere to give you thanks,
Lord, holy Father, almighty and eternal God,
through Christ our Lord.
For on the feast of this awe-filled mystery,
though invisible in his own divine nature,
he has appeared visibly in ours;
and begotten before all ages,
he has begun to exist in time;
so that, raising up in himself all that was cast down,
he might restore unity to all creation
and call straying humanity back to the heavenly Kingdom.
And so, with all the Angels, we praise you,
as in joyful celebration we acclaim:

—Preface II of the Nativity of the Lord, no. 36

Reflection

Christmas is surely an "awe-filled mystery," one that we can grasp to some extent but also one so enormous that much about its meaning escapes us. We spend our whole lives learning not so much about the birth of a Baby so long ago, but about the birth of a Messiah whom we still encounter, who still guides our lives, who still envelopes us with his loving care. This Preface tells us much about this Messiah.

This Messiah is "invisible in his own divine nature." Yes, Jesus was truly God, but he did not cling to that divinity (see Philippians 2:6). When Jesus was incarnated, he "appeared visibly in" our human nature and lived as one of us. He took on everything about our nature except sin. By not clinging to his divinity Jesus showed how much he wanted to identify with our human nature. He could have avoided misunderstanding and rejection, confrontation and anger, suffering and death. But he didn't. He embraced all these in order to conquer them and open the way for our own wholeness, well-being, salvation.

The Nativity of the Lord also shatters our limited understanding of time. When the Messiah was born, he lived in our time, in the unceasing passing of minutes and hours and days and years. He had a past he knew, a present he was living, and a future still open to him. To live in our time he had to let go of the eternity of time with no duration that is proper to God. He was "begotten before all ages" and yet subjected himself to the limitations of our time as duration. Without letting go of eternity, Jesus would not have fully entered into our human nature. Had his divine eternity of time overshadowed his human duration of time, the disciples' being slow to understand him, Pilate's caving to popular pressure, Judas' betrayal would all have just been instances within the larger eternity of triumph. But, no, Jesus experienced all these things in his very humanity and all the disappointment and frustration that we experience when we encounter misunderstanding, weak wills, and betrayal.

Jesus' Incarnation raised all of us up to share in his victory over evil and even death itself. He lived our humanity; he genuinely understands our weakness, our temptations, and our tendency to choose ourselves over faithfulness to God. He "calls straying humanity back" into his saving arms, gives us more chances to be faithful than we can count, and loves us so much when we choose to open ourselves to his Gospel of love. This Messiah is ever the Anointed One of God, who in his risen glory is present to us if we only open ourselves to his love. We celebrate so much more at Christmas than Jesus' birth as a baby so long ago. We celebrate the birth of a Messiah who came to save and to restore the unity of all creation as it was at the beginning of time.

To Ponder

- Jesus not grasping his divinity, but letting go to embrace fully our humanity, means to me that . . .

- The mystery of the Incarnation is awe-filled for me in these ways . . .

Prayer

God of wonder and of love,
the mystery of your divinity is far beyond our understanding,
and yet you invite us into a share in your Divine Life.
As we meditate on the Incarnation of your Divine Son,
help us to come to greater appreciation
for the awesome wonder of being created in the Divine Image.
Help us to be ever more grateful
that the Messiah shared so fully in our humanity
and raised us up to a new dignity.
We ask this through Christ our Lord. Amen.

3.6   LENT AS GRACIOUS GIFT

Roman Missal Text

It is truly right and just, our duty and our salvation,
always and everywhere to give you thanks,
Lord, holy Father, almighty and eternal God,
through Christ our Lord.
For by your gracious gift each year
your faithful await the sacred paschal feasts
with the joy of minds made pure,
so that, more eagerly intent on prayer
and on the works of charity,
and participating in the mysteries
by which they have been reborn,
they may be led to the fullness of grace
that you bestow on your sons and daughters.
And so, with Angels and Archangels,
with Thrones and Dominions,
and with all the hosts and Powers of heaven,
we sing the hymn of your glory,
as without end we acclaim:

—Preface I of Lent, no. 39

Reflection

Some pharmacies have a sign by their prescription counter that informs customers that if they don't like the taste of their medication, the pharmacist can add a flavor. We humans like to sugar coat things that seem unpleasant to us, even if we know they are good for us or help us. For many of us, Lent is another of those unpleasant things we endure. Each year it comes around, we firmly make our resolutions to do something, and then wait for Lent to be over. Some people are even in a bad mood all of Lent because of what they are "giving up." How odd! The Church's liturgical season that is to help turn our lives toward more love and care for others and ourselves becomes for some a season of bad moods that has a negative effect on self and others. Obviously, this is not what the Church has in mind by giving us Lent as a penitential season.

This Preface is most interesting in that it calls Lent "God's gracious gift each year." Doing penance a gift? Now that is surely counterintuitive! Nonetheless, Lent is a gift because we will experience the joy of Easter's new Life according to how well we have opened ourselves to conversion through our acts of penance during Lent. If Lent is just six more weeks of the same way of living, then we cannot anticipate Easter with "minds made pure" through our self-discipline and self-emptying. Lent is a time to help us focus on God as the center of our lives and a time to care for others as a tangible witness to our commitment to God's ways.

The Preface suggests how we spend our Lent, mentioning two of the traditional three prongs of penance. First, we are to be "more eagerly intent on prayer." We notice that it doesn't necessarily tell us to pray more. Many of us already have a well-balanced and healthy prayer life. What this Preface does tell us is that Lent is a time to grow in our prayer intensity, a time to become more eager about encountering our God through attentiveness and openness. God cannot speak to us and guide us if we are not ready to welcome him into our hearts and listen to the encouragement and conversion that God's Presence always brings. Being more eagerly intent on prayer is one sure way to deepen our relationship with God.

We are also to be "more eagerly intent" on the "works of charity." These works are acts of love made visible by our reaching out to care for others. We do not necessarily need to volunteer at some soup kitchen or food pantry (although these are very laudable things to do). Sometimes in our eagerness to help those in need "out there," we forget to heed the needs of those nearest and dearest to us. Perhaps we can spend a bit more quality time with the children or with our spouse. Or we take the time to call a parent or other relative or friend who is in a retirement community or health care center and we know the person is lonely. Or maybe we ourselves are the person in need and we are called by Lent to examine our own all-too-busy lives and give ourselves the rest we need to be wholesome, holy people. In these ways and in countless others, our works of charity deepen our relationship with others. When we reach out with care for others, we ourselves are never the same.

The third prong of penance not mentioned in this Preface, but mentioned in the Gospel for Ash Wednesday, is to fast (see Matthew 6:1–6, 16–18). As with the other acts of penance (prayer and charitable works), fasting is not a marathon to see how much we can deny ourselves. Nor is it a time finally to go on that diet we've been meaning to try in order to lose weight. No, fasting has a much deeper, more religious intent. By fasting and feeling physical hunger, we are reminded to hunger for the spiritual realities that help us grow in "participating in the mysteries." Ultimately, fasting is about being reborn in Christ and emptying ourselves to make room for the fullness of grace that Jesus' dying and rising have brought us.

To Ponder

- If I change my attitude about Lent and its penitential practices, what will happen to me is . . .

- When I examine my daily living, that on which I am most eagerly intent is . . .

- I wish I were more intent on . . .

Prayer

You bestow your gracious gifts upon us, merciful God,
and give us the joy of observing Lent with open hearts and eager wills.
Help us to embrace our Lenten penance
not as something we begrudgingly endure
but as a graced opportunity
to deepen our relationship with you and others.
We ask this through Christ our Lord. Amen.

3.7 THE REALITY OF THE CROSS

Roman Missal Text

It is truly right and just, our duty and our salvation,
at all times to acclaim you, O Lord,
but in this time above all to laud you yet more gloriously,
when Christ our Passover has been sacrificed.
By the oblation of his Body,
he brought the sacrifices of old to fulfillment
in the reality of the Cross
and, by commending himself to you for our salvation,
showed himself the Priest, the Altar, and the Lamb of sacrifice.
Therefore, overcome with paschal joy,
every land, every people exults in your praise
and even the heavenly Powers, with the angelic hosts,
sing together the unending hymn of your glory,
as they acclaim:

—Preface V of Easter, no. 49

Reflection

Everything about the Easter season shouts excess! Consider these two phrases from this Easter Preface: "in this time above all to laud you" and "overcome with paschal joy." Above all and overcome—yes, Easter is a time of excesses. We recognize that Easter brings to fulfillment Jesus' saving mission, and so our response can only be one of praise and thanksgiving. Of all the wonderful celebrations during the liturgical year, Easter is the culmination of all our belief, fidelity, and self-emptying because it is the culmination of Jesus' obedience to his Father's will, his self-emptying serving, and his unending love. We know all this in our heads, but this Preface calls us to feel it in our hearts, too, for we are to be "overcome with paschal joy." Not simply overwhelmed, we are to be *overcome* with exuberant joy. We are to be overtaken, swept off our feet, utterly beside ourselves. We are lifted out of our earthly existence and transported to that realm where "the heavenly Powers, with the angelic hosts, sing together the unending hymn of glory." Jesus' Resurrection is a time of unceasing hymning or praising because no event like this has ever happened in the history of creation and humankind. No one has risen from the dead never to die again. No one has broken the chains of death. No one has so utterly defeated evil. But there is another side to this Easter story.

The Preface reminds us, in the face of all this joy, that "Christ our Passover has been sacrificed." He gave over his body to be scourged and crowned, stripped and nailed to a cross. The "reality of the Cross" is that the road to salvation was paved by the One who offered himself totally for our gain. He "showed himself the Priest, the Altar, and the Lamb of sacrifice."

As Priest, he mediated, with his own body and life, between the depravity of our human condition and the glory he won for us. He is our eternal High Priest (see Hebrews 4:14—5:10) who is the Holy One; he shows us how to be holy, and draws us into his holiness. He ever intercedes for our salvation, leading us along the journey of life toward the fullness of Life shared with him in everlasting glory. He is the mediator who beckons us to be one with him and his Spirit and, through them, one with the Father.

As Altar, the sins of the world are heaped upon him. He receives all our disappointments and discouragements. All our longings and expectations weigh down upon him. He bears all this in silence, our own sacrifice of praise being gathered by him and given over to his Father in heaven. In his continual sacrifice of self-giving, he unites our self-giving to himself as an eternal gift to the Father. He is always with us, never rejects whatever we give him—especially our very selves.

As the Lamb of sacrifice, he is the first to place himself on the altar, to offer his very life for us. Even so, his sacrifice is not a single event of long ago, once and for all done with. No, his sacrifice is a continual self-giving in the Eucharist, a continual offering himself to his Father, a continual giving of himself to us as the Bread of life and Chalice of salvation. We partake of this Lamb of sacrifice and make his sacrifice our own. In this, we are lifted up. By giving over his Body and spilling his Blood, his Life becomes our life.

The "reality of the Cross" is that both death and Resurrection are grounded in life. The reality of the Cross requires of us what it demanded of Jesus: total self-giving for the good of others. The glory of Resurrection is the victory over ourselves.

To Ponder

• For me, the "reality of the Cross" is that . . .

• I am overcome with Paschal joy when . . .

Prayer

God of the cross and of Resurrection,
you raised your Divine Son to new Life,
and in that joyous event
    we ourselves share in the glory of that same Resurrection.
May our thanks and praise be lifted to you
    in an unending sacrifice of ourselves.
Help us to live the Gospel in such a way
that we become ever more worthy
to announce the paschal joy we celebrate.
We ask this through Christ our Lord. Amen.

3.8   Gaze in Wonder

Roman Missal Text

It is truly right and just, our duty and our salvation,
always and everywhere to give you thanks,
Lord, holy Father, almighty and eternal God.
For the Lord Jesus, the King of glory,
conqueror of sin and death,
ascended (today) to the highest heavens,
as the Angels gazed in wonder.
Mediator between God and man,
judge of the world and Lord of hosts,
he ascended, not to distance himself from our lowly state
but that we, his members, might be confident of following
where he, our Head and Founder, has gone before.
Therefore, overcome with paschal joy,
every land, every people exults in your praise
and even the heavenly Powers, with the angelic hosts,
sing together the unending hymn of your glory,
as they acclaim:

—Preface I of the Ascension of the Lord, no. 50

Reflection

Both the angels and the disciples *gazed* as Jesus "ascended to the highest heavens" (Preface; and see Acts of the Apostles 1:10). But these were different gazes. The angels' gaze was one of wonder and worship. They are the ones who stand in the Lord's Presence for all eternity and are the heavenly choir that constantly raises their voices in praise of the Lamb who was slain. On the other hand, in the account of the Ascension in the Acts of the Apostles, "two men in white robes" came to the disciples and asked, "Why do you stand looking up toward heaven?" (Acts of the Apostles 1:11). We might surmise that the disciples were gazing upward to catch a last glimpse of this One they had come to love and follow. Their hearts were probably filled with a combination of wonder, regret, sadness, longing, dismay. Now what? Their leader was gone. They were left alone with the enormous task of continuing Jesus' saving mission. They had been sent out by Jesus when he was still among them to take his message of Good News to others and had been successful (see, for example, Luke 9:1–6; 10:17–20). But Jesus was there to comfort and encourage them when they returned, to debrief and help them understand better what their mission was. Now Jesus is gone. Now what? We have all probably asked the same question, Now what? What does Jesus ask of us?

The Preface helps us understand that, yes, Jesus ascended into heaven but did not and would not leave us orphans (see John 14:18). Jesus remains the "Mediator between God and" us, the risen One who is ever with us through the Holy Spirit. Jesus ascended "not to distance himself from our lowly state" but so the Holy Spirit might come to dwell within us and be the Comforter who guides us in our mission to bring the Good News to all. Jesus' Ascension—his leave-taking—was necessary in order for the Holy Spirit to come and dwell within us. His Ascension paved the way for another kind of Divine Presence, the Holy Spirit whom Jesus promised to send when he appeared to the disciples after his Resurrection (see, for example, John 14:16).

There is another consequence of the Ascension to which this Preface alerts us. By ascending into heaven, Jesus points to where our own faithful journey as disciples leads us. The Ascension gives us the confidence that we will "follow where he, our Head and Founder, has gone before." Jesus' Ascension is a pledge of our own eternal glory. It is a pledge that one day we will rise to be with him in his eternal glory. This festival is one of confidence and joy, manifesting for us where our identifying with Jesus' life and ministry, death and Resurrection leads. We join with all the angels in wonder and awe. We join with all the angels in praise and thanksgiving. We join the entire heavenly choir as we lift our hearts to the One who is victorious and who draws us to share in that same victory.

To Ponder

- My gaze is turned toward . . .

- I am most confident that I will share Jesus' everlasting glory when . . .

Prayer

Almighty God,
you raised your Son from the dead,
and now he sits at your right hand
    where he remains in eternal glory
and judges both the living and the dead.
Instill in us a renewed confidence
that one day we will be with him in Paradise.
Strengthen us to continue his saving ministry
    while we remain here on earth.
We ask this through Christ our Lord. Amen.

3.9   SUMMONED TO A GLORY OF BEING

Roman Missal Text

It is truly right and just, our duty and our salvation,
always and everywhere to give you thanks,
Lord, holy Father, almighty and eternal God,
through Christ our Lord.
For through his Paschal Mystery,
he accomplished the marvelous deed,
by which he has freed us from the yoke of sin and death,
summoning us to the glory of being now called
a chosen race, a royal priesthood,
a holy nation, a people for your own possession,
to proclaim everywhere your mighty works,
for you have called us out of darkness
into your own wonderful light.
And so, with Angels and Archangels,
with Thrones and Dominions,
and with all the hosts and Powers of heaven,
we sing the hymn of your glory,
as without end we acclaim:

—Preface I of the Sundays in Ordinary Time, Ordinary of Mass, no. 52

Reflection

Through Jesus' Paschal Mystery he "accomplished the marvelous deed of our salvation." In this he "freed us from the yoke of sin and death," but this freely given gift also has its cost. We ourselves are to pass over from our sinful way of living, thereby identifying ourselves with Christ and his Paschal Mystery. His Mystery becomes our mystery. This Mystery is about passing from death to risen Life; it is about hearing and responding to the Good News by the way we live; it is about becoming one with Christ, accepting our identity as members of his Body. The Paschal Mystery did not just happen to Jesus nor is it confined to those historical events of long ago. Jesus' Paschal Mystery is a way of living, a way of emptying ourselves of all that is selfish and self-serving and allowing ourselves to be filled with the risen Life of Jesus' Resurrection.

Each Sunday as we celebrate the day of Resurrection, we are summoned by Jesus to offer ourselves in the eternal sacrifice of self-giving. We are to place ourselves on the altar along with the bread and wine, being transformed as they are, into the Body and Blood of the risen Christ. Each Sunday Jesus accomplishes the marvelous deed of giving himself over for our salvation. Each Sunday we offer ourselves with him and become with him a perfect sacrifice of praise and thanksgiving. We are so bold to do this not because of any accomplishments of our own, but because Christ summons us to the same glory of being that his risen Life is.

By immersing ourselves in the Paschal Mystery—in the mystery of self-emptying and exaltation—we become "a chosen race, a royal priesthood, a holy nation," a people of God's very own possession (1 Peter 2:9). We are a chosen race because immersion in the Paschal Mystery makes us members of the Body of Christ. We are the beloved of God. We are daughters and sons of the God whom Jesus revealed to us. We are a royal priesthood because we are the visible Presence of Christ in our world today through the Holy Spirit. That Life within us enables us to mediate the holiness of God's Life and intercede for others. We are priests forever because the Paschal Mystery aligns us with the great High Priest, Jesus Christ. We are a holy nation because, as members of Christ's Body, we are a community of believers who build each other up, who care for others as Jesus cares for us, who draw others through the witness of the goodness of our own living into the one fold of the Good Shepherd who guides us in all things. We are a people of God's very own possession because we are brothers and sisters of the Divine Son. God possesses us with holy jealousy because we are of the Son. God summons us into a unique intimacy with God through the risen Christ and in the power of the Holy Spirit.

Our worship on Sunday can be nothing less than a hearty praise and thanksgiving because this communal act makes present the Paschal Mystery, calls us again and again out of darkness and into God's own wonderful light. Each Sunday we bask in the brilliance of the Resurrection, receiving from God the gift of risen Life.

To Ponder

- The self-emptying and exaltation of the Paschal Mystery means to me . . . , requires of me . . .

- God summons me to . . .

- I am able to respond because my identity with Christ makes me one who is . . .

Prayer

God of wonder and Life,
you summon us to be immersed in the dying and rising
    of the Paschal Mystery of Jesus Christ, your Son and our Lord.
Help us to relish the tremendous gift of self-identity
    this summons bestows upon us.
At the same time, help us to embrace,
    with commitment and fortitude,
the demands of dying to self for the good of others.
We ask this through Christ our Lord. Amen.

3.10   THE SWEETNESS OF GOD'S GRACE

Roman Missal Text

> It is truly right and just, our duty and our salvation,
> always and everywhere to give you thanks,
> Lord, holy Father, almighty and eternal God,
> through Christ our Lord.
> For at the Last Supper with his Apostles,
> establishing for the ages to come the saving memorial of the Cross,
> he offered himself to you as the unblemished Lamb,
> the acceptable gift of perfect praise.
> Nourishing your faithful by this sacred mystery,
> you make them holy, so that the human race,
> bounded by one world,
> may be enlightened by one faith
> and united by one bond of charity.
> And so, we approach the table of this wondrous Sacrament,
> so that, bathed in the sweetness of your grace,
> we may pass over to the heavenly realities here foreshadowed.
> Therefore, all creatures of heaven and earth
> sing a new song in adoration,
> and we, with all the host of Angels,
> cry out, and without end we acclaim:

—Preface II of the Most Holy Eucharist, no. 6

Reflection

This Preface makes clear the connection between the saving memorial of the cross and the Eucharist. In both the cross and the Eucharist Jesus offers himself as a pleasing sacrifice to his Father. In both the cross and the Eucharist Jesus is "the acceptable gift of perfect praise" to his Father. Self-giving in itself is praise of God because self-giving moves us beyond ourselves toward the Other and other. Self-giving conforms us to Christ and makes us "an acceptable gift of perfect praise" to the Father.

Being nourished by the Body and Blood of Christ, we participate in the very holiness of Christ as we become more perfectly one Body in Christ. We are holy because Christ is holy. This holiness is the ground of our unity as a people "bounded by one world" in which we live, is the ground of our one faith whereby we ply ourselves with a firm yes to God's holy will, and is the ground of our being "united by one bond of charity." The holiness and unity made possible by our share in the Eucharist is the mark of those who come to "the saving memorial of the Cross." It is the mark of those who embrace self-giving as a way of living.

In the Eucharist, we receive a foretaste of the glory of the Life to come where we stand forever at the Messianic Table partaking in the delectable Food of God's glorious Presence for all eternity. Here, at this Eucharistic Table, we are "bathed in the sweetness of [God's] grace," a sweetness that washes us in the Blood of the Lamb and prepares us to live in the self-giving of Jesus. This self-giving is not only visible in specific acts of kindness and caring, but is a habit of being that draws us out of ourselves and orients us toward the holiness and Presence of God. This sweetness of God's grace clothes us with the peace and unity of those who are touched by God with the incredible Divine Presence that strengthens and nourishes us to turn toward others who are in need.

The sweetness of God's grace is no saccharin substitute for an easy life that would leave a bitter aftertaste. This sweetness is the pure joy of receiving the risen Son's Body and Blood into our very being and being transformed into living witnesses of the glory of his cross and Resurrection. This wondrous Sacrament is the sign of our unity, our hope, the pledge of the fullness of Life. It is the sign of our self-giving that makes us one in Christ.

To Ponder

- When I meditate on how Eucharist connects the cross and Resurrection, I am moved to . . .

- I experience unity of faith, the one bond of charity, the boundedness of the human family when . . .

Prayer

Wondrous God of the cross and Resurrection,
your Son has given us this Sacrament of the Eucharist
as a perpetual memorial of his self-giving sacrifice on the cross
and the pledge of our participation in his risen Life.
May our full, conscious, and active participation
    in the Eucharistic celebration
bring us the joy and peace of our own self-giving
and strengthen us to be faithful to our identity
as the Body of Christ continuing Jesus' saving mission.
We ask this through Christ our Lord. Amen.

3.11 FROM LOWLINESS TO GREATNESS

Roman Missal Text

> It is truly right and just, our duty and our salvation,
> to praise your mighty deeds in the exaltation of all the Saints,
> and especially, as we celebrate the memory of the Blessed
>   Virgin Mary,
> to proclaim your kindness as we echo her thankful hymn of praise.
> For truly even to earth's ends you have done great things
> and extended your abundant mercy from age to age:
> when you looked on the lowliness of your handmaid,
> you gave us through her the author of our salvation,
> your Son, Jesus Christ, our Lord.
> Through him the host of Angels adores your majesty
> and rejoices in your presence for ever.
> May our voices, we pray, join with theirs
> in one chorus of exultant praise, as we acclaim:
>
> —Preface II of the Blessed Virgin Mary, no. 63

Reflection

We call Mary the Mother of God, our Mother, the Blessed Virgin, the pure spouse of St. Joseph, she who was conceived immaculately, she who is full of grace, she who was taken body and soul into heaven. These are all exalted ways of addressing and thinking about Mary. What this Preface emphasizes, however, is "the lowliness of [God's] handmaid." Mary is most holy because she freely chose to be the servant of God. She said yes to what God asked of her, not knowing what suffering she herself would embrace, not knowing who her Son would be, not knowing how much she would have to let go in order for this Divine Son to be about his ministry of salvation.

Mary's lowliness is not about her being poor or ignorant or with no influence. Quite the opposite. Mary was rich in grace. She was rich in her relationship to God, for she trusted that what God asked of her would lead to all people receiving God's "abundant mercy from age to age." She was rich in that people, even to the ends of the earth, would come to know and venerate her, love and call upon her to intercede with her Son for our needs. Nor was Mary ignorant. She was wise to question how she could conceive while a virgin, and yet said yes. She was wise to trust that her Son would respond to a mother's concern and change water into wine. She was wise to put her grief aside and stand at the foot of the cross, never abandoning her Son and always being there as a mother to bring him hope and consolation.

Mary's lowliness is not about self-abasement, but about humbly accepting to cooperate with God in the great things God did through her for us. Mary nurtured Jesus' human life, and by becoming incarnate Jesus is the "author of our salvation," the source of our Life and holiness, from whom all good things flow. As Mary spent her whole life growing into God's plan for our salvation, she models for us the way we must spend our lives discerning God's will for us. She encourages us to be faithful in our own yes to whatever God asks and begs us to unite ourselves with her in echoing our thankful hymn of praise to God the Creator and Redeemer.

On festivals of Mary—and, indeed, every day—we venerate Mary for embracing the lowliness that brought her to greatness. This lowliness is the greatness of choosing to be a servant of God and of all who come to her for her help, kindness, and consolation. Her lowliness inspires all of us to be God-bearers as she was, to be servants of holiness, to be great in all the things we do for God who makes it possible.

To Ponder

- I think about Mary when . . . She inspires me to . . .

- I am faithful in my yes to God as was Mary when I . . .

- I fall short of Mary's yes when I . . .

Prayer

Saving God,
you chose the handmaid Mary
to bear your Divine Son in her womb,
nurturing his life and guiding him
    as only a holy Mother can do.
Help us to imitate Mary's humility,
to be open to the Presence of her Divine Son,
and to be willing to say yes to our disciple-service
as we draw on her for comfort and strength.
We ask this through Christ our Lord. Amen.

3.12   STAND FIRM

Roman Missal Text

> It is truly right and just, our duty and our salvation,
> always and everywhere to give you thanks,
> Lord, holy Father, almighty and eternal God,
> through Christ our Lord.
> For you have built your Church
> to stand firm on apostolic foundations,
> to be a lasting sign of your holiness on earth
> and offer all humanity your heavenly teaching.
> Therefore, now and for ages unending,
> with all the host of Angels,
> we sing to you with all our hearts,
> crying out as we acclaim:
>
> —Preface II of Apostles, no. 65

Reflection

Most things that are purchased today have a built-in obsolescence. Electronic items are outdated almost as soon as they are carried out the store. Appliances go bad within a decade. Clothes barely last a season. We have become a throwaway society, and with this state of affairs comes an attitude of impermanency, fleetingness, devaluation. Even with medical advancements improving our life expectancy, we still know that in the whole scheme of things we are but a blip on the radar screen. This Preface counters this state of affairs and brings us back to consider what is most permanent in our lives.

The Church has existed since Christ. That is over two thousand years! No nation, no government, no institution has endured as long as the Church. Yes, things in the Church have come and gone. At one time, the Church was made up of semi-independent communities of faithful, committed followers of Jesus who gathered regularly around their community leader for prayer and worship; we are too large for that now. At one time, the Church owned no public buildings, but simply gathered in family homes for their prayer and worship; we are too large for that now. At one time, the Church had no formal laws, but only the law of the Gospel; we are too large for that now. Perhaps precisely because we are so large now, things have not only changed but have also expanded and grown. At one time, the Church officially only named two sacraments (Baptism and Eucharist); overtime, she came to name the seven we celebrate today. At one time, the Church's service to the poor was primarily directed to their own members in need; now we are a large charitable community reaching out to Catholics and others all over the world with many kinds of services to whoever is in need. At one time, we depended upon the priest for all our spiritual needs; now we have many lay people who are well-formed to serve us through various ministries.

Through all the changes in the Church over these past two thousand years, there have been constants, and these are what ensure that the Church will last. The Church is built on "apostolic foundations." This means that the Gospel preached by Jesus, taken up by the Apostles, and handed down through the ages still forms our values and convictions. The Apostles walked with Jesus, were taught by him, were sent forth by him to preach and heal as he did. We trace our roots to the Apostles and build upon their witness of fidelity and truth. Further, the Church is a "lasting sign of [God's] holiness on earth." This means that, as Christ promised, he would be with us until the end of time (see Matthew 28:20). What directs the Church is the risen Christ's gift of the Holy Spirit. The Spirit who dwells within and among us is the assurance of the truth of the Church as well as the holiness of the Church. The Spirit is the assurance that the Church will last "now and for ages unending." Finally, the Church offers all humanity the "heavenly teaching" that Jesus came to announce. The adjective "heavenly" is a telling one here. The Church only teaches what comes from God and is ordained by God. We are God's Church, and that is why the Church will last "now and for ages unending."

Though we are divinely inspired and guided by the Holy Spirit, we may be uncomfortable and even upset with some of the history of the Church. But the Church is still very much a human institution. The mistakes and failures are our own; mistakes happen when we do not listen to the Holy Spirit's teaching and do not follow the Holy Spirit's guidance. Even in spite of our failures, the Holy Spirit assures that the Church will last "now and for ages unending." This is an encouraging message of this Preface. In the Church, the Body of Christ, we are united with our risen Lord through the Spirit in such a way that we cannot fail. We will last forever.

To Ponder

- I am most encouraged by the Church when . . .

- I am most discouraged when . . .

- That the Church is built upon apostolic foundations and guided by the Holy Spirit means to me . . .

Prayer

Triune God, Father, Son, and Holy Spirt,
you are present in your Church
and guide us in all truth.
Help us to be open to your heavenly teaching
and to be faithful to the law of love
that binds us into your holy people.
We ask this through Christ our Lord. Amen.

3.13　FIRM RESOLVE

Roman Missal Text

It is truly right and just, our duty and our salvation,
always and everywhere to give you thanks,
Lord, holy Father, almighty and eternal God.
For you are glorified when your Saints are praised;
their very sufferings are but wonders of your might:
in your mercy you give ardor to their faith,
to their endurance you grant firm resolve,
and in their struggle the victory is yours,
through Christ our Lord.
Therefore, all creatures of heaven and earth
sing a new song in adoration,
and we, with all the host of Angels,
cry out, and without end we acclaim:

—Preface II of Holy Martyrs, no. 69

Reflection

It was not uncommon in the early Church to call the baptized faithful "saints." For example, Paul begins his Letter to the Philippians with these words: "To all the saints in Christ Jesus . . . " (Philippians 1:1). Generally speaking, the saints are the holy ones of God. In this sense, Abraham, Moses, Ruth, and Esther from the Old Testament are saints. Some saints we canonize; this means that the Church officially recognizes some holy women and men as saints, as models of holiness for us to imitate. This Preface points to a particular kind of saint: the martyrs.

From the very beginning of the Church, the martyrs have warranted special recognition by Christians. Their absolute fidelity to the Gospel and resoluteness in following Christ brought them suffering and death as he endured. In this fidelity and resoluteness, they were perfectly conformed to Christ—in his life, sufferings, death, and Resurrection. Their sufferings are wonders of God's might, not because God wants us to suffer, but because suffering and death witness to the power of God's invitation to holiness. Suffering and death witness to the power of the Gospel to attract and hold us, and to the energy of the Holy Spirit that gives ardor to our faith and "firm resolve" to withstand the falsehood and emptiness of the lures of evil. Out of faithful suffering and death, God brings the victory of fullness of Life for all eternity.

When we honor the martyr-saints, we honor their lives, their Gospel way of living, the truth of God's mighty Word, the grace of God's gift of Self to us. In honoring the martyr-saints, we glorify and praise God because they have made visible in their lives God's will and gifts. The honor never stops with just the martyr-saints, but always goes beyond them to the God whom they loved so zealously and served so faithfully.

Sometimes the martyrs seem to be so far beyond us. They seem to have a hold on holiness that isn't quite normal. Nonetheless, when we read the lives of the martyrs we find that they really lived simple lives. But they did so heroically. We do not need to do big things to be a saint. We only need to do everything for God's honor and glory, according to God's will, for the good of all. The canonized saints include martyrs and popes, bishops and kings, great teachers and preachers. But the list of canonized saints also includes mothers and fathers, sons and daughters, those who could neither read nor write, those who were physically deformed, those who were very young. Saints come from all walks of life. But what they all have in common is great love for God and others, a burning desire to be faithful to whatever Jesus asks, and an openness to whatever circumstances they found themselves in. Holiness is lived everywhere.

To Ponder

- My favorite saint is . . . because . . .

- Martyrs inspire me in these ways . . .

- I am aware that my own life glorifies God when I . . .

Prayer

Holy Father, almighty and eternal God,
you have before your Divine Majesty
    the whole company of martyrs and saints
    who never cease to give you praise.
Draw us to their goodness and fidelity
so that one day
we will join them in the fullness of Life,
giving you everlasting praise.
We ask this through Christ our Lord. Amen.

3.14 AT GOD'S SUMMONS

Roman Missal Text

It is truly right and just, our duty and our salvation,
always and everywhere to give you thanks,
Lord, holy Father, almighty and eternal God.
For it is at your summons that we come to birth,
by your will that we are governed,
and at your command that we return,
on account of sin,
to the earth from which we came.
And when you give the sign,
we who have been redeemed by the Death of your Son,
shall be raised up to the glory of his Resurrection.
And so, with the company of Angels and Saints,
we sing the hymn of your praise,
without end we acclaim:

—Preface IV for the Dead, no. 81

Reflection

This Preface names both the reality of the human situation and the hope we receive at our Baptism by our incorporation in the Body of Christ. It is at God's "summons that we come to birth." We have been the beloved of God since even before we were knit in our mother's womb (see Psalm 139:13). Our human life is a gift from God. However, "on account of sin" we do not receive the life God originally gave our first parents, Adam and Eve, but a life that has lost some of its original gifts.

Notably, we are mortal; we will die; we will return to that earth from which we came. Although we are governed by God's will, the free will that God gave us at our birth allows us to accept or reject that divine will. When we accept God's will and surrender ourselves to God's plan for our happiness, we grow in Life and holiness. But sometimes we do not accept God's will and put distance between ourselves and God, harming the most Life-giving relationship we have.

God could have created us without free will. Life does not need free will. But since God did choose to create us in the divine image, God also desires that we live by more than the instincts of our animal nature. We are beings who can discern right from wrong, who can see fit to reach out to others sometimes even at our own expense, who can delay our own gratifications in order to gain something of higher value. All this is exercise of our free will. When we choose God's ways, we are exercising rightly our free will. Then we give God great praise and honor.

Even when we are largely faithful to God and constantly grow in our loving relationship with God and each other, all of us must face our own mortality. One day each of us will die, each of us will pass from this earthly existence as we know it. Suffering in its many forms, and mortality, is our human inheritance as those descending from Adam and Eve. But we still have hope. Christ conquered death (see Romans 6:9; 1 Corinthians 15:54–57). And since we participate in Christ's death by our Baptism, so do we receive the pledge of rising with him in his Resurrection (see Romans 6:3–4). We "have been redeemed by the Death" of the Son. This redemption opens the door for us to share in Christ's everlasting glory. For those of us who follow Christ, our human death is the door onto Eternal Life. Christ's death conquers mortality. We die only to live forever.

Our hope for immortality that has its foundation in Christ's death and Resurrection does not take away the sting of human suffering and death. It does give it a context that reminds us there is more to this life than we can presently experience. The "more" is one day being "raised up to the glory of" Christ's Resurrection. Yes, we have fleeting moments of this glory now. Those times when God seems so near to us, so caring, so loving. Those times when the solution to something we've been grappling with for a long time suddenly is clear. Those times when we conquer temptations and remain faithful to what we know deep down in our very being is God's will and plan for us. We grieve at the death of a loved one at the same time that we rejoice in the immortal Life that God then bestows on God's beloved faithful ones. Death is both sorrow and joy. Death is an end and beginning. Death is the welcome of God's greatest gift: fullness of Life forever.

To Ponder

- The reality of my human situation is . . .

- What gives me hope is . . .

- What makes my hope in one day sharing in the glory of Christ's Resurrection something real for me is . . .

Prayer

God of life and death,
you will that all of us one day
share in the glory of your Son's Resurrection.
While we trod along on our earthly journey,
ease our pain and suffering,
give courage to our faltering wills,
and help us support one another in the hope of Life everlasting.
We ask this through Christ our Lord. Amen.

3.15   HOLY, HOLY, HOLY

Roman Missal Text

> Holy, Holy, Holy Lord God of hosts.
> Heaven and earth are full of your glory.
> Hosanna in the highest.
> Blessed is he who comes in the name of the Lord.
> Hosanna in the highest.
>
> —no. 31

Reflection

Each Preface concludes with this song of the angels—so called because when Isaiah the prophet had his vision of God in the Temple at his call, angels were in attendance before God singing, "Holy, holy, holy" (Isaiah 6:3). The winged Seraphs were emphatically acknowledging who God is—the Holy One. In the Old Testament, repetition indicates importance, emphasis, something not to be missed. It is not enough simply to call God holy. By crying out "Holy, Holy, Holy" we are recognizing and announcing God's holiness beyond compare, God's being beyond measure, God's majesty beyond telling.

God is holy: "For I am the LORD your God; sanctify yourselves therefore, and be holy, for I am holy." (Leviticus 11:44). Our own holiness derives from God's holiness, God's very being. Our praises ring out because God has desired that we actually share in the holiness that belongs to God alone. We can cry out "Holy, Holy, Holy" as the first of the three acclamations during the Eucharistic Prayer because we are beside ourselves in gratitude, in thanksgiving for God's beneficence in drawing us into the Divine Life, the divine holiness. The Lord is God of the heavenly host. A host is a large number, in later usage applied to an army. The heavenly host is the army of angels and saints who give God glory and praise unceasingly. The Scriptural use of a military term here also references the fact that God is King of the whole universe, that God has great power, that God commands a great army not to conquer others but to invite others into God's ineffable Presence. The fullness of God's glory is reflected by the fullness of the heavenly host's and our "Holy, Holy, Holy."

Hosanna in the highest. *Hosanna* is one of those Hebrew words that we do not translate because it is so difficult to capture in another language the depth and fullness of its meaning. *Hosanna* has the same Hebrew root as *salvation*, which means "wholeness," "health," and "well-being." We sing here that our well-being is found in the God, who dwells on high. We sing "Hosanna in the highest" to our God, who is Creator and the Source of all life and holiness.

Blessed is he who comes in the name of the Lord. The last part of this acclamation of praise, which comes from Psalm 118:26, places us in a Messianic context. In the Psalm, it is uttered in a thanksgiving liturgy celebrating Israel's victory over an enemy. The whole Psalm sings of salvation—health and wholeness and well-being have come to Israel through the defeat of enemies by God's power and might. This is the same verse on the lips of the crowd when Jesus triumphantly entered Jerusalem seated on a donkey (see Matthew 21:9; Mark 11:9–10; Luke 19:38; John 12:13). All four Evangelists record this incident and these words. The irony here is that Jesus' victory does not come in being hailed as the Son of David, the Messiah, when he enters Jerusalem, but his victory comes when he dies and is raised up in the Resurrection. Salvation comes when our Messiah-King seems anything but a powerful God who has dominion over all the heavens and earth. Yet we know who this Messiah is. We know he sits in the highest heavens at the right hand of God. We know he is the One who continually gives himself to us on this altar as our heavenly Food. We repeat our "Hosanna in the highest," acclaiming Jesus' power and might, his victory over evil and death. As Jesus said to Pilate, his kingdom is not of this world (see John 18:36). Not even the heavenly host came to his defense. Yet, an angel did minister to him at his time of need to give him strength (see Luke 22:43). The heavenly host serves God and is a multitudinous army protecting and guiding us in right ways and also leading us in singing "Holy, Holy, Holy Lord God of hosts." Our acclamation reveals that "heaven and earth are full of [God's] glory."

- The times outside of the Eucharistic liturgy that my heart is raised in an acclamation of "Holy, Holy, Holy" in praise and thanksgiving to God are . . .

- I become aware that the heavenly host protects and guides me when I . . .

Prayer

Lord God of hosts,
your might is unequaled
and your power lifts us up to share in your glory.
Receive our acclamation of praise
    from hearts overflowing with gratitude
    for your countless gifts to us.
Make us worthy to sing your praises
and help us be fitting followers of your Son,
the King, Messiah, and Redeemer.
We ask this through Christ our Lord. Amen.

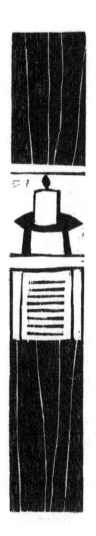

CHAPTER 4

Texts Drawn from the Eucharistic Prayers

The Eucharistic Prayer is our great thanksgiving. We ask God to send down the Holy Spirit to bless and sanctify the gifts of bread and wine so that they may be changed into the very Body and Blood of our Lord Jesus Christ. We also ask God to send the Spirit to make us one Body, so that we are changed into being more faithful followers of Jesus who continue his saving mission. With him, we offer ourselves to God as a fitting sacrifice. By our thanksgiving we respond to Jesus' command at the Last Supper to "Do this in remembrance of me" (Luke 22:19). We also pray for all members of the Church, living and dead, and look forward to receiving the fullness of Life of which the Eucharist is both pledge and promise. Our prayer must be fervent, heartfelt, and loving.

4.1 THESE HOLY AND UNBLEMISHED SACRIFICES

Roman Missal Text

> To you, therefore, most merciful Father,
> we make humble prayer and petition
> through Jesus Christ, your Son, our Lord:
> that you accept
> and bless ✚ these gifts, these offerings,
> these holy and unblemished sacrifices,
> which we offer you firstly
> for your holy catholic Church.
> Be pleased to grant her peace,
> to guard, unite and govern her
> throughout the whole world,
> together with your servant N. our Pope
> and N. our Bishop,
> and all those who, holding to the truth,
> hand on the catholic and apostolic faith.
>
> —Eucharistic Prayer I, no. 84

Reflection

We begin Eucharistic Prayer I with a clear statement of how we ought to approach our merciful Father: we come to God with humble prayer. Humility is not self-abasement; instead, it is an acknowledgment of who we are in God's eyes. It is an acknowledgment of God's greatness and our status as creatures. It is an acknowledgment of our limits and mortality in face of God's infinite goodness and eternal Life. Humility, however, does not bid us to pray with timid hearts.

How amazing it is that we even dare approach our God! This is the One who made us and all of creation. This is the One who gives us life and abundance. This is the One whom we approach with our petitions, fully confident that God graciously gives us even more than we dare ask. This God never tires of our petitions, never grows weary of our pleas for mercy, and never refuses to accept what we offer from grateful and humble hearts. We dare to offer, because the Divine Son so graciously offers Self continually for us. Jesus' sacrifice on the cross—his very sacrifice of Life—is made present for us at each Eucharistic sacrifice. Likewise, his risen life is given to us as our heavenly food and drink.

Although we usually think of *sacrifice* in rather negative terms (giving up something), the root of this word means to "make sacred." Whatever part of ourselves and our possessions we render to God, we do so not to placate an angry God, but to come nearer to a God who wishes to make us sacred, make us holy. This holiness is a share in God's very Life.

During our celebration, we unite ourselves with Jesus, who is the perfect offering, the "holy and unblemished" sacrifice. By such union, we ourselves become part of the offering, part of the "holy and unblemished" sacrifice. By giving ourselves over as Jesus did, we continue a long tradition of handing on the Catholic and apostolic faith. Faith is not simply assent to truths (that is, doctrine), but it is assent to Truth, the Divine Word, who teaches us all things in the depths of our hearts. Jesus' life and ministry was one of utter self-giving; so must our life be. In the Eucharistic Prayer we learn that manner of self-giving because there we encounter Jesus in his supreme sacrifice of life for our salvation.

The negative aspect of sacrifice—giving up or, better, giving over—opens the way for the positive aspect of sacrifice—being made sacred, holy. By imitating Jesus' giving over, we become more like him; we become living sacrifices offering ourselves to the merciful Father for the peace and good of the whole world.

To Ponder

- I experience God as merciful most often when . . .
- Humility helps me give over in that . . .
- To be a living sacrifice means to me . . .

Prayer

Merciful Father,
you sent your Divine Son to be a living sacrifice for our salvation.
Help us to give ourselves over for the good of others
in the same way Jesus modeled giving over
    by his life, death, and Resurrection.
Strengthen us to be more faithful followers
so that we ourselves become living sacrifices
sharing in the risen Life of the Divine Son.
We ask this through that same Son, Jesus Christ our Lord. Amen.

4.2   GIFTS BORNE TO THE DIVINE MAJESTY

Roman Missal Text

> In humble prayer we ask you, almighty God:
> command that these gifts be borne
> by the hands of your holy Angel
> to your altar on high
> in the sight of your divine majesty,
> so that all of us, who through this participation at the altar
> receive the most holy Body and Blood of your Son,
> may be filled with every grace and heavenly blessing.
>
> —Eucharistic Prayer I, no. 94

Reflection

For many of us, the first prayer we learned as tiny children was the prayer to our guardian angel. We were taught that each of us when born was given by God a special angel to watch over us, to guard us, and to help us when in trouble. We also know that angels are God's messengers. It was the archangel Gabriel who came to Zechariah to announce that he and his barren wife Elizabeth would bear a child whom they were to name John. This same Gabriel also appeared to Mary to announce to her that she would conceive by the Holy Spirit and bear a Son, whom she should name Jesus. The heavens were filled with a multitude of angels, who announced this wondrous birth and sang out their "Glory to God in the highest heaven, and on earth peace among those whom he favors" (Luke 2:14).

As wonderful as these guardians and messengers are, angels have another even more significant reason for being. Neither human nor divine, they are God's creation, who are ever before the divine majesty singing God's praises:

> And all the angels stood around the throne . . . , and they fell on their faces
> before the throne and worshiped God, singing, / "Amen! Blessing and glory
> and wisdom / and thanksgiving and honor / and power and might / be to our
> God forever and ever! Amen." (Revelation 7:11–12)

And . . . and . . . and. Can we ever stop joining our voices with the heavenly choir before the throne of God singing praises to the One beyond all creatures, yet the One who cares so much for us?

How fitting it is for us humbly to beg God to send a holy angel to bear our gifts to God's altar on high! The angels stand before the Divine Majesty always. As faithful guardians of us, they will steadfastly bear these gifts to God. As faithful messengers, they will bear our own meager song of gratitude and praise, uniting it with theirs so that there may be a thunderous cry of jubilation before the Divine Majesty. Along with the gifts, we ourselves are borne by the holy angel to God's throne, where we are privileged to share in the "most holy Body and Blood" of our Lord Jesus Christ.

How reassuring it is to us to have angels ever so close to the Divine Majesty to bear our gifts and ourselves along with them to be in the Divine Presence! As they never lose sight of the Divine Majesty, so may we never lose sight of God's Presence, God's Gifts, God's Life. The angels bid us to turn our whole being toward the Divine Majesty, to unite ourselves with the offerings of bread and wine so that we, too, may be borne on high.

To Ponder

- I join the heavenly choir in singing God's praises unceasingly when I . . .

- I experience being borne to God's altar on high when . . .

Prayer

O Divine Majesty,
you deserve all honor and glory, thanks and praise.
May we always join our voices
to those of the heavenly choir
to sing of your mighty deeds
and praise you for your untold goodness.
We ask this through Christ our Lord. Amen.

4.3   SPIRIT LIKE THE DEWFALL

Roman Missal Text

> You are indeed Holy, O Lord,
> the fount of all holiness.
> Make holy, therefore, these gifts, we pray,
> by sending down your Spirit upon them like the dewfall,
> so that they may become for us
> the Body and ✚ Blood of our Lord Jesus Christ.
>
> —Eucharistic Prayer II, nos. 100–101

Reflection

It often seems like water is not where it's supposed to be when it's supposed to be. One year in one place there is terrible, life-threatening, and crop-destroying drought. In the same year in another place, there may be life-taking and property-ravaging flooding, either too much water or not enough. We humans need water, but we need it just so. We bow to water's force and beg when water is scarce.

Such a beautiful water image the beginning of Eucharistic Prayer II uses! We beg God to send the Holy Spirit upon the gifts "like the dewfall." Neither deserts nor rainforests harbor dewfall. Dew happens only when time and place are just so. Dew forms when the heat of the day meets the coolness of the night. Dew forms when the air is pregnant with moisture bursting to rain down on the just and unjust alike (see Matthew 5:45).

It is very rewarding to rise early on a summer's morn and experience the dewfall. It permeates everything. It does not choose this blade of grass or that flower petal, but covers everything. It sparkles like the stars at night, winking at us a promise of new life, new growth, and new possibilities. Without tasting, it tastes cool, refreshing, and inviting. It bids us to put off our sandals and simply embrace the glory of God's creation and holiness (see Exodus 3:5). Dew reminds us that we stand on holy ground when we step out of ourselves and into the Life that God promises.

When we beg God to send down the Holy Spirit upon these gifts like dewfall, we are praying that the Holy Spirit do to the bread and wine as the dewfall does to the parched summer green: enliven these gifts with new Life, the very Being of the Divine Son. The Holy Spirit comes down upon these gifts and changes them from mere creature-made goods into the very Body and Blood of our Lord Jesus Christ. From the "fount of all holiness"—the very Being of God—these gifts of bread and wine are made holy, made into the very substance of the risen Son. Our partaking of these changed gifts is a partaking in the "fount of all holiness." These gifts transform us from standing on holy ground to being holy ground ourselves.

As the Holy Spirit comes upon the gifts like dewfall, there is also a challenge for us. As the Holy Spirit permeates the gifts, so must we permeate our lives, our world with the risen Life given us by this same Holy Spirit. As the dewfall sparkles with the promise of new life, so must we shine forth the risen Life that is within us. As the dewfall covers everything, so must our goodness be a mantle over all those we meet. As the dewfall cools and refreshes, so much we put out the fires of indifference and hatred and bring instead the refreshing balm of compassion and forgiveness.

To Ponder

- The image of dewfall says to me . . .
- The Holy Spirit comes over me when . . . I am empowered to . . . I am changed because . . .

Prayer

Send forth your Holy Spirit upon us, O Holy Lord, like the dewfall.
May it refresh and enliven us
so that we might more perfectly be the Presence of your risen Son
    for all those we meet each day.
May the Life of the Holy Spirit imbue us with renewed courage
to live the Gospel with fervor and ardor.
We ask this through Christ our Lord. Amen.

4.4   WORTHY TO BE ONE WITH CHRIST

Roman Missal Text

> Therefore, as we celebrate
> the memorial of his Death and Resurrection,
> we offer you, Lord,
> the Bread of life and the Chalice of salvation,
> giving thanks that you have held us worthy
> to be in your presence and minister to you.
> Humbly we pray
> that, partaking of the Body and Blood of Christ,
> we may be gathered into one by the Holy Spirit.
>
> —Eucharistic Prayer II, no. 105

Reflection

Memories are an important part of all of our lives. Our family's special days and civil holidays are all about remembering important events. We keep an abundance of photos; the digital photo frames have become popular gifts, especially for grandparents. We can load literally thousands of pictures into them for constant viewing. In all these cases, however, the memories are of past events or experiences and remain in the past except in our memories. When we make memorial in the Eucharistic Prayers, we are not simply recalling the past. Rather, we are drawing the past event into the present, making it as fruitful now as at its first occurrence.

We celebrate the memorial of Jesus' death and Resurrection each time we celebrate liturgy. This means that the full power of Jesus' overcoming evil and death and ushering in risen Life not only for himself but also for us to share is an ongoing, real event for us. Our memorial makes present in the here and now the consequences of Jesus' life and utterly faithful obedience to his Father. Our Eucharistic praying draws us into this same event—and constantly connects us with our Baptism when we are first plunged into this sacred and saving Mystery (see Romans 6:3–4).

Our response to this invitation to be so united with Jesus in his saving Mystery can only be giving thanks, which is what we do during the Eucharistic celebration. Our union with Jesus makes us worthy to stand in the presence of so great a Mystery, to offer ourselves along with Jesus to the Father, and to receive back the gifts of bread and wine that now are the "Bread of life and Chalice of salvation." This is no ordinary offering, no ordinary gift, no ordinary return. During Eucharist our thanks is marked and made concrete by our giving ourselves over to God in our whole being; we offer ourselves. The gifts of bread and wine are enlarged by the very gift of ourselves. When we receive God's return of the gifts, now transformed, we ourselves eat and drink and become more perfectly united with Jesus in his saving Mystery. We, too, continually give ourselves over to dying to self so that we receive from the hand of God the gift of fullness of Life.

This gift-exchange is not possible, nor are we worthy, by our own efforts. Our task is to surrender ourselves and let God work in and through us. Closely associated with the memorial is a second invocation or prayer of the Holy Spirit, now called upon ourselves as gifts offered. We pray that the Holy Spirit come down upon us and gather us into one Body in Christ. It is the power of the Holy Spirit that enables such a close union with Christ; it is the Spirit who enables us to share in his death and Resurrection; we share in his self-offering and risen Life. We must surrender to the Holy Spirit and the gift of renewing ourselves in Christ. For such do we always and everywhere give thanks!

To Ponder

- God's never-ending gifts to me include . . .

- I am most able to express my heartfelt gratitude when . . .

- Uniting myself more perfectly with Jesus' death and Resurrection means that I must . . .

Prayer

Redeeming God,
your Son Jesus accepted death and received from you risen Life.
We are invited to share in this same holy Mystery
    by offering ourselves to you
as a living gift of our love and gratitude.
Make us one in the Body of Christ
and strengthen us to serve worthily
    all our sisters and brothers
in the communion of the Body.
We ask this through Christ our Lord. Amen.

4.5 FROM THE RISING OF THE SUN TO ITS SETTING

Roman Missal Text

> You are indeed Holy, O Lord,
> and all you have created
> rightly gives you praise,
> for through your Son our Lord Jesus Christ,
> by the power and working of the Holy Spirit,
> you give life to all things and make them holy,
> and you never cease to gather a people to yourself,
> so that from the rising of the sun to its setting
> a pure sacrifice may be offered to your name.
>
> —Eucharistic Prayer III, no. 108

Reflection

When we were largely an agrarian society, and especially before the advent of electric lights, the sun's rising and setting much more clearly marked the beginning and ending of our days. There was a natural rhythm to our days determined by darkness and light. During the long days of light, the planting and harvesting were done. During the shorter days of light, repairing of implements and rest occurred. Thus, there was not only a daily rhythm of light and darkness, but also a seasonal rhythm of work and rest. This rhythm permeated everything that was done.

In Eucharistic Prayer III, we pray "that from the rising of the sun to its setting a pure sacrifice may be offered." This is an image for unending sacrifice, an image suggesting that sacrifice permeates all our days, all our lives. By implication, all creation rightly gives God praise because all creation is filled with the gift of life and holiness from God. Our sacrifice makes us sacred, and calls us uniquely into God's presence. No matter the time of day—in both darkness and light—our whole being is called to give God thanks and praise. Perhaps even the psalmist recognized how God permeates all our days when he prayed, "My soul is satisfied as with a rich feast, / and my mouth praises you with joyful lips / when I think of you on my bed, / and meditate on you in the watches of the night" (Psalm 63:5–6). Even the darkness of night and sleep cannot keep us from turning toward our God with praise.

But there is another meaning in this image of rising and setting sun. The synoptic Gospels tell us that it was at the sun's rising when Jesus' Resurrection was discovered (though not yet understood) (see Matthew 28:1; Mark 16:1; Luke 24:1).

The rising sun awakes us to a new day to live in the light. Jesus' Resurrection is associated with this new day, new light. It was the first day of the week when Jesus rose—a day we came to call Sunday, but just as well we could call it "Sonday."

John uses different imagery. He reports that Mary Magdalene came to the tomb "Early on the first day of the week, while it was still dark" (John 20:1). The divine act of Resurrection occurred in the darkness of night, when all but the watchers of the night were asleep, oblivious to God's mighty act of life-giving. God's risen life-giving pushes aside darkness and all the evil and death that is associated with it.

By praying that "from the rising of the sun to its setting a pure sacrifice may be offered," we are praying that our days are permeated with the very Mystery of Jesus' death and Resurrection. In darkness, we enter into the death of sleep so that we can rise at the new day refreshed and ready to continue Jesus' saving ministry. Our whole lives are to be a pure sacrifice of obedience to God's will and gratitude for the Life-gift that God offers us. Just as the rising and setting sun marks a natural rhythm to our days, so does the death and Resurrection of the Son mark a spiritual rhythm for how we live in Christ.

To Ponder

- As metaphors, light and darkness mean to me . . . suggest to me that . . . call me to . . .

- The rhythm of my days looks like . . .

- The rhythm of Christ's death and Resurrection permeates my days when I . . .

Prayer

Glorious God of day and night,
you permeate our days with your Divine Presence and gift of Life.
Help us to live the rhythm of Christ's dying and rising faithfully,
so that we might one day share
in the glory of the fullness of risen Life he gained for us.
We ask this through Christ our Lord. Amen.

4.6   CONSTANT INTERCESSION

Roman Missal Text

> May he make of us
> an eternal offering to you,
> so that we may obtain an inheritance with your elect,
> especially with the most Blessed Virgin Mary, Mother of God,
> with your blessed Apostles and glorious Martyrs
> (with Saint N.: the Saint of the day or Patron Saint)
> and with all the Saints,
> on whose constant intercession in your presence
> we rely for unfailing help.
>
> —Eucharistic Prayer III, no. 113

Reflection

Younger folks might express their life goals in terms of a successful job, financial security, a good marriage, dream vacations, owning a beautiful home. Middle age folks might express their life goals in terms of living near their grandchildren and seeing them often, traveling the world, and sufficient retirement funds. The elders among us might express their life goals in terms of maintaining health, having family near, and being able to stay in their own home. Beyond these normal human life goals, our spiritual selves desire eternal happiness with God in heaven. We live our entire spiritual lives with this one primary goal in mind. All the Eucharistic Prayers mention those who have gone before us and truly do enjoy the fullness of Life with God forever.

In Eucharistic Prayer III, we pray that we may obtain an inheritance with God's elect. The notion of elect means someone chosen, set apart. We are God's elect because God has chosen us to be beloved daughters and sons; we are also God's elect because we choose God as the center of our lives and strive to do God's holy will faithfully. As God's elect, we already share in God's Divine Life, we already are saints. We count ourselves among the holy ones, among the elect. From the very beginning of the Church, further, we have enumerated in our liturgies those among us whom we recognize as models of holiness.

The first among the saints is the "most Blessed Virgin Mary, Mother of God." We also call her the first among the disciples. From even before Jesus' birth she nurtured him in her womb, she prepared to bring him into this world, she nurtured him so he would grow in wisdom and stature and age (see Luke 2:52). She was the one who pushed him into public life when she was so concerned about a potentially embarrassed newlywed couple running out of wine for their wedding feast guests (see John 2:1–12). She too stood beneath the cross of her dead Son (see John 19:25). No doubt she was among the disciples in the Upper Room when Jesus appeared to them after the Resurrection (see John 20:19–23), although she is not specifically named to be among the disciples. Might Jesus have appeared to her when alone, assuring his beloved mother that he had risen?

The Apostles and martyrs are mentioned as two special groups of saints. The Apostles, of course, were those Twelve whom Jesus had personally chosen to follow him on his earthly journey to Jerusalem and his death and Resurrection. The martyrs have always been a special kind of saint, for they were faithful in following Jesus even to the point of submitting their very lives for the sake of the Gospel. We add a most general group—all the Saints. We beg these elect—these who have already won the crown of righteousness, the crown of life, the crown of glory (see 2 Timothy 4:8; James 1:12 and Revelation 2:10; 1 Peter 5:4)—to intercede for us. These saints are in God's Presence; they see God face to face. They are the faithful ones. Surely, whatever they ask of God on our behalf will be granted. We rely on them for unfailing help. Constant in God's Presence, they are constant in their intercession for us. Having preceded us in death, they nevertheless love us and continually care for us. Our Mother in heaven, our sisters and brothers in heaven will never fail us. They wish for us the eternal joy they have obtained. We can have no better intercessors before God's throne.

To Ponder

- My favorite saints are . . . because . . .

- Mary teaches me these things about her Divine Son . . .

- I am most confident when praying to the saints that my needs are made known and heard before God when I . . . This brings me great comfort in that . . .

Prayer

Ever-living and loving God,
the company of the faithful elect
    constantly stand before your Divine Majesty
and offer praise for your great glory.
Hear the prayers of our Blessed Mother
and all the saints for our needs,
that we may be strengthened to be faithful as they are
and one day share in their company in eternal glory.
We ask this through Christ our Lord. Amen.

4.7   THE FULLNESS OF TIME

Roman Missal Text

> And you so loved the world, Father most holy,
> that in the fullness of time
> you sent your Only Begotten Son to be our Savior.
> Made incarnate by the Holy Spirit
> and born of the Virgin Mary,
> he shared our human nature
> in all things but sin.
> To the poor he proclaimed the good news of salvation,
> to prisoners, freedom,
> and to the sorrowful of heart, joy.
> To accomplish your plan,
> he gave himself up to death,
> and, rising from the dead,
> he destroyed death and restored life.
> And that we might live no longer for ourselves
> but for him who died and rose again for us,
> he sent the Holy Spirit from you, Father,
> as the first fruits for those who believe,
> so that, bringing to perfection his work in the world,
> he might sanctify creation to the full.
>
> —Eucharistic Prayer IV, no. 117

Reflection

Ask small children how much they love their mommy or daddy, and they often spread their arms as wide as can be reached and respond, "This much." For these wee little ones, the spread of the arms is probably not more than a yard. Not very much by adult standards. But we fully understand the intention—the children are stretched to the limits of their reach, to the limits of their imagination. When we think about how God loves the world, there really is no limit. God's arms stretch out to embrace the entire universe, all our world, all our imagination, all our possibilities, all our being. God's love has no limits. This kind of unfathomable love is made visible in the Only-Begotten Son who took on our human flesh and was like us in all things except sin. Well, perhaps he was not like us in love either, for Jesus' love was perfect and stretches as far as does divine love to embrace all in his grasp, all in his saving work.

Jesus' becoming incarnate by the Holy Spirit ushered in "the fullness of time" a new way of being, and a new way of becoming. Through the power of the Holy Spirit, not only was Jesus incarnated in the womb of the Virgin Mary, but also by the power of that same Holy Spirit, he is incarnated under the signs of bread and wine on the altar, here in our midst. The "fullness of time" is now as we share in this sacred Mystery. The "fullness of time" is now as we join ourselves to Christ's offering of Self.

The "fullness of time" also occurs in our daily living when we imitate Jesus' life and ministry. Eucharistic Prayer IV includes a kind of blueprint for Christian living. While reciting the works of Jesus' ministry, we are also rehearsing our own ministry. To the "poor he proclaimed the good news of salvation;" we ourselves are to announce the wholeness and well-being that life in Christ offers to whoever comes our way. Everyone who has not heard the Good News of salvation is poor. The Good News of salvation also calls us to reach out to those who lack food and shelter, family and friends, gainful work and peace of heart.

Jesus proclaimed freedom to prisoners. He is the new Moses, who beckons us to leave whatever slavery binds us—slavery to our own self-centeredness, to wanton desires for more and more things, to choosing what harms us over God's will, which frees us. We are all prisoners when we let anything at all get in the way of freely choosing God to be the center of our lives. It is so easy to become imprisoned in our own small world and close ourselves off to the goodness and needs of others. We free ourselves when we reach out beyond the narrow confines of our own limited imagination and allow God to work wonders through us. This is ultimate freedom: allowing God to take hold of us and direct our lives beyond where we might go and be ever surprised by what we discover there.

Jesus proclaimed joy to the sorrowful of heart. Sorrow of any kind weighs us down. Even when our sorrows are of our own making—we make too many commitments and get bogged down in doing rather than being; we have heavy hearts because our unreasonable ambitions are not fulfilled; we mourn the loss of family and friends—God comes to us with the healing balm of Divine Presence. Joy is not the absence of sorrow; rather, joy is the fullness that comes from casting our cares on God, knowing so well that God is always there to hold us up.

In the "fullness of time," Jesus destroyed death and restored Life. In this rhythm of self-emptying and Life-gift, Jesus opens to us the wonder of salvation. In this rhythm, Jesus calls us to trust in his risen Presence and mercy, to have hope that we do share in his risen Life, and to believe that he never forsakes us. When we open ourselves to Jesus, take on his life and ministry, and proclaim the same Good News as he did, we ourselves already live in the "fullness of time." Jesus' death and Life is our death and Life. Thus is the "fullness of time" now.

Prayer

Loving God,
in the "fullness of time" you sent your Divine Son to live among us
and show us the way to a share in risen Life.
May we live as he did,
reaching out to others
with self-giving, compassionate, and joyful hands.
Strengthen us to bring to completion his saving work.
We ask this through Christ our Lord. Amen.

4.8 HEAVENLY INHERITANCE

Roman Missal Text

To all of us, your children,
grant, O merciful Father,
that we may enter into a heavenly inheritance
with the Blessed Virgin Mary, Mother of God,
and with your Apostles and Saints in your kingdom.
There, with the whole of creation,
freed from the corruption of sin and death,
may we glorify you through Christ our Lord,
through whom you bestow on the world all that is good.

—Eucharistic Prayer IV, no. 122

Reflection

One of the wonderful pleasures of parenthood is seeing the children grow up into happy, healthy, successful adults. In our present age of scattered families, all too often the adult children live far from their parents. Skyping and texting make frequent communication somewhat easy, yet as wonderful as these modern conveniences are they still fall short of personal presence. What parent or child does not lament absence at the high feast days and holidays? How many Christmas song lyrics mention being home for the holidays? How difficult it is for so many of our military personnel to be far from home during special family celebrations! How heartwarming it is for all of us to see news reports of a military father or mother surprising a child with an unexpected Christmas or birthday homecoming! The children cannot contain themselves—they run and leap and jump into the waiting parent's arms—arms outstretched to the limit in welcome.

We are God's children, and so we await our heavenly inheritance. God's mercy overlooks our faults and failings. We look forward to the Life after death when we are "freed from the corruption of sin and death." Meanwhile, during this liturgy, we already have a foretaste of heaven. We come to the banquet table where God nourishes us with the very Body and Blood of the Divine Son who conquered evil and put to death death. The Blessed Virgin Mary and all the Apostles and Saints are with us here during this liturgy and accompany us on every step of our journey toward our heavenly inheritance. God comes to us with the divine arms outstretched to the limit in welcome, even now. Even now, God shows us divine mercy, invites us to share in a foretaste of our heavenly inheritance, and frees us to be children of the light. Even now, God embraces each of us tightly and wants never to let go.

Sometimes adult children comment that their parents have become their best friends. They share with them their innermost confidences, their deepest dreams and aspirations, and sometimes even still hear from them parental guidance and correction. So it is with us children of God. In the words proclaimed, in the prayers uttered, in the saints whom we invoke, we are learning how to be God's children; how to grow into God being our best friend; and how to listen, learn, and become who God calls us to be.

To Ponder

- I most deeply yearn to be in God's Presence when . . .

- I find that Presence here . . .

- My friends show me how God is my Divine Friend when they . . .

Prayer

God of mercy and love,
you call us your children, and so we are.
May we grow into our heavenly inheritance
    by listening to you in your word
    and through each other.
May the trust and fidelity and constancy
of our friendships with each other
lead us to a friendship with you that satisfies and nourishes,
that brings us joy and contentment,
that teaches and admonishes us to become ever more perfectly
    the children you desire us to be.
We ask this through Christ our Lord. Amen.

4.9 ARMS OUTSTRETCHED BETWEEN HEAVEN AND EARTH

Roman Missal Text

You are indeed Holy, O Lord,
and from the world's beginning
are ceaselessly at work,
so that the human race may become holy,
just as you yourself are holy.
Look, we pray, upon your people's offerings
and pour out on them the power of your Spirit,
that they may become the Body and ✚ Blood
of your beloved Son, Jesus Christ,
in whom we, too, are your sons and daughters.
Indeed, though we once were lost
and could not approach you,
you loved us with the greatest love:
for your Son, who alone is just,
handed himself over to death,
and did not disdain to be nailed for our sake
to the wood of the Cross.

But before his arms were outstretched between heaven and earth,
to become the lasting sign of your covenant,
he desired to celebrate the Passover with his disciples.

—Eucharistic Prayer for Reconciliation I, nos. 2–3

Reflection

To reconcile means to bring what is estranged back into fruitful relationship. The opening lines of the Eucharistic Prayer for Reconciliation I remind us that while it is wholly our work to estrange ourselves from God (that is, commit sin), it is God's unceasing work to bring us back into God's loving embrace. We must acknowledge our sinfulness, while it is God who forgives. We must desire to repair a weakened or broken relationship, while it is God who reconciles. We must desire to overcome weaknesses and grow in holiness, while it is God who freely gifts us with Divine Life, with holiness. Even when we are hesitant to come to God, God reaches out to us in ways we cannot even imagine.

When we are lost, God still loves "us with the greatest love." God's love is not like our human words of love, sometimes so shallow and fleeting. God's love is a permanent Divine Word spoken to us in the wonder of the Incarnation and the life and ministry of the Divine Son. This same Son accepted all our humanity, all our weaknesses, all our suffering, even human death—Jesus was like us in all things except sin. Jesus, being all-holy himself, never chose to estrange himself from his Father, for he and his Father are one (see John 17:11). In Jesus, God's embrace is expansive and lasting.

During the Eucharistic celebration we make present the lasting sign of God's covenant, the visible and continuing self-giving of the Divine Son. Jesus cements our relationship with his Father. He did so on the cross. This symbol of his total self-giving is a lasting sign of God's love, God's mercy, God's unceasing desire for our reconciliation. Jesus' arms were "outstretched between heaven and earth" on the cross. His stretched and nailed arms and hands embraced all the weakness of God's children in such an act of self-giving that heaven and earth were reconciled, became one in the Divine Father's mercy-love. The self-giving on the cross is the antecedent of the self-giving of the Eucharist. The arms "outstretched between heaven and earth" is the antecedent of the warm embrace of reconciliation.

To Ponder

- What estranges me from God and the Life and holiness God offers me is . . .

- The image of Jesus' arms "outstretched between heaven and earth" stirs up in me . . . moves me to reconciliation with God and others in that . . .

Prayer

God who is mercy and compassion, love and forgiveness,
hear our cries to be one with you,
to be received into your loving embrace.
Reconcile us with each other
as we strive to create a human community
    patterned after the Life-giving love
that is your Life in the Holy Trinity.
When we stray from your embrace,
awaken us to the truth of our sinfulness
and help us turn back to you.
We ask this through Christ our Lord. Amen.

4.10   OUR PASSOVER AND SUREST PEACE

Roman Missal Text

Therefore, as we celebrate
the memorial of your Son Jesus Christ,
who is our Passover and our surest peace,
we celebrate his Death and Resurrection from the dead,
and looking forward to his blessed Coming,
we offer you, who are our faithful and merciful God,
this sacrificial Victim
who reconciles to you the human race.
Look kindly, most compassionate Father,
on those you unite to yourself
by the Sacrifice of your Son,
and grant that, by the power of the Holy Spirit,

as they partake of this one Bread and one Chalice,
they may be gathered into one Body in Christ,
who heals every division.

—Eucharistic Prayer for Reconciliation I, no. 7

Reflection

All of us during our life have many times when we pass over from one thing to another. Little ones pass over from being at home or kindergarten to entering the first grade. Adolescents pass over from grade to high school. Eighteen-year-olds pass over from high school to college or job. Some people pass over from being single to married. Others pass over to the clerical or religious state. We pass over from unemployment to employment, from employment to retirement. Each of these and many other times we pass over from one thing to another. A change happens to us and makes a difference in who we are and how we are. But no pass over we embrace has near the importance of our passing over into God's Life. During liturgy, as we celebrate the Passover of Jesus Christ, we celebrate also our own life in him, our own passing over from death into risen Life.

Our entry into Jesus' Passover is a union with Christ that is at the same time a union with the Father and Spirit. His Sacrifice is our sacrifice; his Self-giving is our self-giving; his obedience is our obedience. By uniting ourselves with Christ in all of his life, suffering, death, and Resurrection we become more perfectly his Body, become more perfectly a living Sacrifice that continually brings God glory.

We pray that we might "partake of this one Bread and one Chalice." "One" here goes beyond the practical sign of a single loaf or cup; it points to the unity we share in the Body of Christ because we eat of the food given us from the Messianic Banquet Table. We eat and drink and we become what we eat and drink. This food is a gift of the Father's compassion, the Son's continual Self-giving, and the Holy Spirit's power exercised for our gain. We gain God's Life, but more. We gain oneness with the Holy and Almighty God that is our surest peace. This peace is far more than tranquility and freedom from alienation. This peace is the state of our own embrace of Jesus' Passover, which means it is a commitment to hand ourselves over to God.

Raising the issue of Jesus' Passover in our Eucharistic praying always reminds us that at this highest point of our week (Sunday Mass), this time of peace in God's Presence, we are also faced with its cost. The way to risen Life is through death. The way to the exaltation of risen Life is through self-emptying. The way to union with our Triune God is through surrender of ourselves. One important reason for also partaking of the Cup of Blood at Communion is that we are reminded through a wonderful and tangible way that our life is about the joy of celebrating Christ's victory over death, but it is also about our own willingness to spill our own life-blood—our very selves—for the sake of others. We drink from the Cup of Blood and celebrate the blood of the cross that flowed from Jesus' side and called us to be Church.

Wine has a side effect of breaking down inhibitions, unleashing joy, and marking celebration. While we obviously don't drink enough of the Precious Blood to physically feel these effects, nonetheless our partaking of the Chalice of salvation does open us more readily to the utter self-giving and consequent happiness that come from uniting ourselves in such a way with our Savior. His Life-Blood courses through our own bodies, transforming us ever more perfectly into living sacrifices that make visible his constant love for us.

To Ponder

- The peace I experience when giving myself over for another's good is . . . This peace is sure when . . .

- My own passing over from self-giving to the exaltation of risen Life illustrates . . .

Prayer

Compassionate God,
your Divine Son embraced the cross
and so opened the door for us to enter into the fullness of Life.
May we worthily eat of his Body and drink of his Blood
so that we might have the sure peace of his Presence and love.
We ask this through Christ our Lord. Amen.

4.11   HAND EXTENDED TO SINNERS

Roman Missal Text

> You, therefore, almighty Father,
> we bless through Jesus Christ your Son,
> who comes in your name.
> He himself is the Word that brings salvation,
> the hand you extend to sinners,
> the way by which your peace is offered to us.
> When we ourselves had turned away from you
> on account of our sins,
> you brought us back to be reconciled, O Lord,
> so that, converted at last to you,
> we might love one another
> through your Son,
> whom for our sake you handed over to death.
>
> —Eucharistic Prayer for Reconciliation II, no. 2

Reflection

The sweet Jesus often depicted in religious art does not represent his true physical characteristics. The son of Joseph was a carpenter like his foster father (see Mark 6:3). Jesus was used to hard physical labor that made him physically strong. He worked splintering wood with his hands. His hands were no doubt rough and calloused. Can't we just picture him finishing a piece of furniture for his mother, and gently caressing the grain of the wood, the smoothness resulting from his sanding, relishing in the magnificence of this product of nature and his own labor to be a gift to his beloved mother?

In the second Eucharistic Prayer for Reconciliation, he is the "Word that brings salvation," as well as the "hand" God extends to sinners. When Jesus extends his hand to us, it is with strong attraction and sure grip. Jesus wants to grasp us in these Laborer's hands and never let go. He wants to take us to himself and bring us the peace that can only be known by those who are gently nestled in his strong arms and hands. Even when we turn away from God "on account of our sins," Jesus does not forsake us but extends the beckoning hand of reconciliation that once again unites us with him and his Father through the power of the Holy Spirit.

It is always a heart-warming picture to see a father and child out for a walk, hand in hand. The father is more than twice as tall as the child. He reaches down as the child reaches up to be grasped. In that hand is security and love, assurance and protection, guidance and security. So it is with Jesus who reaches down to grasp our own hand when we have strayed. All we need do is turn to him, reach up, and grasp his hand to once again be assured that we are treading the right path toward fullness of Life rather than the destruction that comes from turning away from God.

What love the Father has to hand "over to death" the Only-Begotten Son! This love does not desire that the Son suffer, but that the Son do all that is necessary to reconcile us sinners with God and each other. The one thing necessary is union with God, effected by conformity to God's will. Sin is straying from doing God's will, quitting the hand that ever reaches out to us in mercy, compassion, and love. When we do not allow ourselves to be grasped by Jesus' hand, we are left without the sure guidance necessary to stay in union with him and his Father. We are left empty-handed. We are left utterly alone. Jesus never withdraws his hand of reconciliation; all we need do is reach up and let him grasp us with his strength and love. Only then can we reach out a hand of reconciliation to each other, and "love one another" as he loves us.

To Ponder

- I feel the strength of Jesus' hand grasping me when . . .

- I am most impelled to reach out with the hand of reconciliation to another when . . .

Prayer

Strong and compassionate God,
you extend your Divine Son to us
    as a hand that grasps us in mercy
    and embraces us with love.
Help us to reach up and take that hand by our own,
    never to let go,
always to be open to wherever the Son leads us.
When we turn away from you and stray,
move us quickly to grasp Jesus' hand
and once again become one with you.
We ask this through that same Christ our Lord. Amen.

4.12   ACCEPT US ALSO

Roman Missal Text

Celebrating, therefore, the memorial
of the Death and Resurrection of your Son,
who left us this pledge of his love,
we offer you what you have bestowed on us,
the Sacrifice of perfect reconciliation.
Holy Father, we humbly beseech you
to accept us also, together with your Son,
and in this saving banquet
graciously to endow us with his very Spirit,
who takes away everything
that estranges us from one another.
May he make your Church a sign of unity
and an instrument of your peace among all people
and may he keep us in communion
with N. our Pope and N. our Bishop
and all the Bishops
and your entire people.

—Eucharistic Prayer for Reconciliation II, no. 7

Reflection

Peer and social pressure are formidable foes. They often take us where we do not wish to go, but the thought of exclusion often sends us helter-skelter into all kinds of situations. The drive for acceptance is so strong in us. We are very uncomfortable when others correct, face us with our own weaknesses or ineptitude, insist we are wrong about something. We don't like the feeling of being other, unconnected with those whom we respect or admire or love. Yet through sin we turn our faces away from God, stray from the path of righteousness, ignore God's overtures of love and gentleness. Often it is the catalyst of losing acceptance among our human peers that brings us to beg God to accept us.

Our prayer to God for acceptance is quite bold, in spite of our humbly beseeching God. The boldness is twofold. First, our bold prayer implies that our cry for acceptance is linked to God's acceptance of the Son, whom God could never reject because Jesus is of the very Being of God. Jesus is God. We are bold in this linking—accept the Son, accept us who are united with him in his Body. If we are to pray so boldly, then we must do what is necessary to grasp God's reaching out to us as God reaches out unfailingly to the Son. We must ourselves become a "Sacrifice of perfect reconciliation" as was Jesus. Reconciliation is a beautiful gift offered to us by God, but it is a gift demanding a response. God does not close the divine eye to our straying from our identity as the Body of Christ. We are a pure sacrifice when we turn ourselves once again toward Jesus and the Gospel he revealed, uniting ourselves with him in his death and Resurrection. Praying for acceptance demands that we unite with Jesus in all his obedience to his Father and the human consequences of that fidelity. We stray when we are not willing to be obedient as was Jesus, when we want the Life God offers without embracing the death.

Second, our bold prayer for acceptance begs God to "endow us" with the Holy Spirit. The Spirit is Life—we are asking God for Life! Reconciliation cannot be gained by our efforts alone. The chasm of alienation is too wide. By opening ourselves to the Spirit who dwells within us, we condition ourselves to let go of our own need for our kind of acceptance and welcome instead the acceptance that only God can give. This "Spirit takes away everything that estranges us." Our sharing in the saving banquet is our own self-emptying and surrender, allowing the Holy Spirit to wash us clean of all alienation from God and each other, nourishing us for the task of unity in Christ. This is our Christian calling: to overcome alienation and become one in Christ. The Gospel roots us in the ministry of reconciliation because we cannot be accepted by God or each other at the same time that we put ourselves and our own needs before all others. The work of the Spirit in and through us is what is reconciling, is what opens us to the acceptance from God and each other that we so desire. Come, O Holy Spirit!

To Ponder

- I feel most accepted by others when . . . most alienated when . . .

- I feel most accepted by God when . . . most alienated when . . .

- Reconciliation means to me . . . I am most able to bring it about when . . .

Prayer

Holy Father,
you accept us even when we are so imperfect,
are so prone to stray from you.
Reconcile us to yourself and each other,
and help us to have hearts filled with gratitude
for your loving mercy and compassion.
We ask this through Christ our Lord. Amen.

4.13   THE JOURNEY OF LIFE

Roman Missal Text

> You are indeed Holy and to be glorified, O God,
> who love the human race
> and who always walk with us on the journey of life.
> Blessed indeed is your Son,
> present in our midst
> when we are gathered by his love,
> and when, as once for the disciples, so now for us,
> he opens the Scriptures and breaks the bread.
> Therefore, Father most merciful,
> we ask that you send forth your Holy Spirit
> to sanctify these gifts of bread and wine,
> that they may become for us
> the Body and ✚ Blood
> of our Lord Jesus Christ.
>
> —Eucharistic Prayer for Use in Masses for Various Needs, nos. 2–3

Reflection

It is comforting to know that God "walks with us on the journey of life." Even when we are not aware of God's Presence, God is still with us, beside us, within us. Each Person of the Holy Trinity loves us in a special way: the Father is ever creating us anew, the Son is ever redeeming us from all alienation, and the Holy Spirit is sanctifying us in ever new and refreshing ways of Life. Their care for us is unbounded and all-embracing. No aspect of our human existence escapes God's divine desire to love the human race to our fulfillment. Nor are we left to our own devices for direction along our journey of life. Jesus has shown us the way.

Recalling the journey of the two disciples on the road to Emmaus after Jesus' Resurrection (see Luke 24:13–35), we pray that we be gathered by Jesus' love as "he opens the Scriptures and breaks the bread." First to be noticed here, is that these are Jesus' actions. The priest stands in our midst as the visible icon of the risen Jesus whose sacrifice we are making present: his Word which we are proclaiming, his Body that is broken again and again for us on this altar.

In the Lukan account of the journey to Emmaus, Jesus does not reveal himself to the two disciples immediately. He meets them where they are—discussing the events of the past days in Jerusalem and trying to discover what they missed, what happened that their hopes were dashed that this One was truly the Messiah whom they awaited. But he died. He is gone. So they thought. Oh, yes, it had been reported that some saw Jesus even after three days of being in the tomb. But who can believe this? Patiently, Jesus walks them through the Scripture passages that foretold who the Messiah would be. These passages must be interpreted in the light of these new events. But they can only be rightly interpreted with an encounter with the risen Lord.

The two disciples came to recognize Jesus in the breaking of the bread. When they recognized Jesus, he vanished. The encounter had happened. Now they were able to discern a new, risen Presence in the breaking of the bread. This encounter caused them to return to Jerusalem to seek the other disciples and report that they had seen the risen Lord. The marvelous thing about this breaking of the bread is that it continues into our own time and place where we ourselves can encounter the risen Lord in the breaking of the bread.

Each Eucharistic celebration has two tables: of the Word, of the Sacrament. It is through the Word that we first are drawn along the journey of life; it is the inspired Word that continues Jesus' timely teaching about how his disciples are to live and minister; it is the Word that constantly challenges us to deeper Gospel living, which determines the path of the journey of life that we are to choose. The Word, then, is given new life through the Sacrament of the breaking of the bread. In the bread and wine sanctified and changed by the power of the Holy Spirit, we once again encounter the risen Lord, come to belief in the Life that our journey promises, and are nourished to choose faithfully the right path that leads to our one day sharing in the fullness of the risen Christ's glory.

To Ponder

- I experience God's tremendous love for me and the whole human race when . . .

- Jesus opens the Scriptures and breaks the bread of Life for me when . . .

Prayer

Holy and loving God,
you never cease to reveal to us your Presence in Word and Sacrament.
Open us to your loving care,
draw us to your Divine Presence,
and lead us along our journey of life
so that one day we may share the fullness of Life with you forever.
We ask this through Christ our Lord. Amen.

4.14   LIFE IN THE SPIRIT

Roman Missal Text

> By our partaking of this mystery, almighty Father,
> give us life through your Spirit,
> grant that we may be conformed to the image of your Son,
> and confirm us in the bond of communion,
> together with N. our Pope and N. our Bishop,
> with all other Bishops,
> with Priests and Deacons,
> and with your entire people.
> Grant that all the faithful of the Church,
> looking into the signs of the times by the light of faith,
> may constantly devote themselves
> to the service of the Gospel.
> Keep us attentive to the needs of all
> that, sharing their grief and pain,
> their joy and hope,
> we may faithfully bring them the good news of salvation
> and go forward with them
> along the way of your Kingdom.

> —Eucharistic Prayer for Use in Masses for Various Needs, III:
> Jesus, the Way to the Father, no. 7)

Reflection

Life in the Spirit means that we live the life of the risen Lord. We are "conformed to the image" of the risen Son. Since the Ascension, we are the "faithful of the Church" who proclaim by our very being and the way we live that Jesus has risen and remains present among us. To be faithful to this tremendous responsibility and privilege of discipleship, we must do two things: discern the "signs of the times" and be "attentive to the needs of all." This was Jesus' life. It is now our life. We are not alone, however, in shouldering the yoke of Jesus' life and ministry. He walks with us through the Holy Spirit, who dwells within us. It is not our life we are called to live, but Life in the Spirit.

Sometimes when we reflect on the signs of the times, we can fall into the trap of only looking at all the things and events around us that have a negative impact on the way we strive to live. Our world is anything but whole. We hear every day about natural catastrophes, hate-induced wars, rampant crime, the ravishment of the environment, increasing poverty. These hit us over the head because they are so obvious. Discernment of the signs of the times must also bring us to look deeper. Living in the image of the Son means that we must notice the person in spiritual pain, those who are alone and isolated, and the person who needs a listening ear. These and countless other signs of pain cry out for our response.

At the same time, discerning the signs of the times helps us notice all the things and events around us that speak of Christ's victory over death and evil. The selfless pastoral associate in our parish might inspire us to volunteer for a ministry. The beauty of a garden might invigorate us to form a committee to plant a community vegetable garden. The glee and abandon of children at play in a park might encourage us to reach out with joy and hope to those who might need a bit more of these virtues in their lives. There is much beauty and good around us. Discerning this can strengthen us to tackle the needs of our families, parishes, neighborhoods, communities, and nation.

Life in the Spirit helps us be "attentive to the needs of all," especially those among us who are most unfortunate. There are always Church and public calls for help for others. And to these calls we all must respond to the best of our ability. At the same time, we must open our eyes to needs that are closer to home. We "share the good news of salvation" when we reach out with a helping hand to someone carrying a heavy load, when we open our hearts to someone without friends, when we are generous with our time and talents. Jesus showed us the way to this kind of living when he reached out with compassion and care to all who surrounded him. We show how we have been "conformed to the image" of the risen Jesus each time we act as he did toward others. When we bring joy and hope to others, our own joy and hope is increased.

To Ponder

- The "signs of the times" that surround my daily life are . . .
  I live in the Spirit when I respond to them by . . .

- I find it most difficult to reach out to those in need
  when . . . I find it easiest to reach out to others when . . .

Prayer

Almighty Father,
you send the Spirit of your risen Son to dwell in us,
to conform us more perfectly to his image,
and to help us live and minister as he did.
May we find joy in reaching out to others in need,
and satisfaction in knowing we have helped them
along their journey to fullness of Life in you.
We ask this through Christ our Lord. Amen.

4.15   PERFECT FAITH AND CHARITY

Roman Missal Text

Look with favor on the oblation of your Church,
in which we show forth
the paschal Sacrifice of Christ that has been handed on to us,
and grant that, by the power of the Spirit of your love,
we may be counted now and until the day of eternity
among the members of your Son,
in whose Body and Blood we have communion.
Bring your Church, O Lord,
to perfect faith and charity,
together with N. our Pope and N. our Bishop,
with all Bishops, Priests and Deacons,
and the entire people you have made your own.
Open our eyes
to the needs of our brothers and sisters;
inspire in us words and actions
to comfort those who labor and are burdened.
Make us serve them truly,
after the example of Christ and at his command.
And may your Church stand as a living witness
to truth and freedom,
to peace and justice,
that all people may be raised up to a new hope.

—Eucharistic Prayer for Use in Masses for Various Needs, IV:
Jesus, Who Went About Doing Good, no. 7)

Reflection

Perfection is a goal not achieved by our own means, but only by the grace of God.
When we pray in this Eucharistic Prayer that God bring the Church to "perfect
faith and charity," we are acknowledging that only God can lead us along the journey of life toward the fullness of Life. Here and now, we strive to be people of faith
and charity. This Eucharistic Prayer makes this very concrete: we are to "stand as
a living witness to truth and freedom, peace and justice." We usually associate
assent to Creed and Tradition with faith, and acts of kindness with charity, and
this is true. But more is required of us. To be a living witness to the Gospel, we
must be generous in serving and faithful in acting.

Jesus' whole life was a witness to bringing "comfort to those who labor and are burdened." He healed the sick, forgave the sinner, included the outcast, taught seekers, challenged the haughty. He met each person where they were and drew them farther along the path toward salvation. Encounters with him always precipitated a choice: to stay with him or leave. Alas, some did choose to leave. But for over two millennia men and women of every race and nation have faithfully chosen to follow Christ on the way to "perfect faith and charity" by reaching out to others as he did.

Perfect faith and charity are grounded in truth and freedom, peace and justice. Truth: what God has revealed to us, particularly in the very Person of the Divine Son. Freedom: choosing to have God as the center of our lives, motivating us to live the Gospel. Peace: the inner calm and steely conviction that come from following the path that Jesus has opened up for us, a path that leads to fullness of Life. Justice: working to form the right relationships that reflect the union and love of the inner Life of the Trinity. All of this turns our life away from ourselves and toward God, drawing us out of ourselves to live the Gospel as Jesus taught.

Perfect faith and charity are not goals we can achieve. They are a way of life that God calls us to live, and this is possible only because the Spirit dwells within us. Our task as followers of Jesus is to listen to that Spirit, to discern what is asked of us, and to witness diligently to God working within us to bring creation and all humanity to completion.

To Ponder

- My faith looks like . . . My charity looks like . . .

- I am most aware of God working in and through me when . . .

- What happens when I surrender myself to God working in me is . . .

Prayer

Redeeming God,
you sent your Son
so that we might learn how to live in "perfect faith and charity."
We know that on our own
we can never live this life,
but with the graciousness of the gift of the Holy Spirit
    who dwells within us,
we can witness to the Good News of the Gospel
and come to the fullness of Life you offer.
Our hearts are filled with gratitude
that you have called us to this marvelous Gospel life.
We ask this through Christ our Lord. Amen.

CHAPTER 5

TEXTS DRAWN FROM THE BLESSINGS

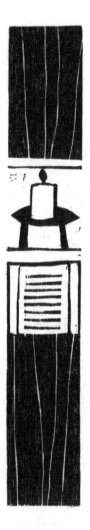

Before Jesus ascended into heaven, he raised his hand and blessed the gathered disciples (see Luke 24:50). Before we are dismissed to live the Eucharist we have just celebrated, we are blessed, too. We are Jesus' disciples who continue his saving work. This blessing sends us forth to be the favor of God, bringing God's kindness and help to all we meet. The blessing at the Concluding Rites of Mass reminds us that all we are and all we have are gifts from God. Part of every blessing, then, is returning gratitude to God for all God gives us. Sometimes a simple form of blessing occurs:

"May almighty God bless you, the Father, and the Son, ✚ and the Holy Spirit."

At other times, a triple invocation or a solemn prayer precedes the blessing over the people.

5.1   Run the Race

Roman Missal Text

> May the almighty and merciful God,
> by whose grace you have placed your faith
> in the First Coming of his Only Begotten Son
> and yearn for his coming again,
> sanctify you by the radiance of Christ's Advent
> and enrich you with his blessing.
> R. Amen.
> As you run the race of this present life,
> may he make you firm in faith,
> joyful in hope and active in charity.
> R. Amen.
> So that, rejoicing now with devotion
> at the Redeemer's coming in the flesh,
> you may be endowed with the rich reward of eternal life
> when he comes again in majesty.
> R. Amen.
>
> —Blessings at the End of Mass, 1. Advent

Reflection

Hamsters are rodents, but they are nonetheless often found in elementary school classrooms and homes where they delight children with their activity. A typical cage has a wheel on which the hamster runs and runs, making the wheel spin and spin. This is an apt image for some of our lives, as we feel ourselves in a rat race. We run and run, spin and spin, and never seem to come to an end of the activity that drives us. This blessing for Advent includes the image of running the race of this life. But this race is not spinning in circles. It is moving toward a clear end: "the rich reward of eternal life."

This blessing helps us know how to live the race of this life without falling into the trap of a rat race: we are to be "firm in faith, joyful in hope, and active in charity." Faith is our yes to God's will for our lives; hope is embracing with all our being the end for which we strive (fullness of Life with God); charity is living our faith-yes and making visible our hope-striving as we reach out in love and care for others. We are able to live in this way because Christ is present to us in so many comforting ways.

At the "First Coming of [the] Only Begotten Son," Jesus showed us so well how to say yes to his Father's will. He himself was obedient in taking on human flesh; he was obedient in revealing through his teaching and preaching the ways of God; he was obedient when others tempted him with the earthly trappings of kingship, and instead in obedience he chose the throne of the cross. For this constant obedience Jesus was raised to new Life, overcoming the lure of selfishness and self-will and evil and even death itself. Our own obedience to God's will, our daily expression of faith, is in imitation of Jesus' obedience, and for this we receive the same risen Life that Jesus himself was given.

At Jesus' Second Coming, when he comes again in glory, our hope for a share in the fullness of his risen Life will be fulfilled. At the same time we await the fullness to come, we already share in its delights now. Advent is filled with joyful expectation of Christ's Presence to us here and now, not simply as a past memory or a future expectation. And so now we are called to live as Christ would, to be active in charity as Jesus was during his life here on earth. We run the race of life through the lens of firmness in faith, joyfulness in hope, and active in charity, for this is the only way that this race of life becomes a steady journey toward the fullness of Life rather than an endless circle of hopelessness and futile activity. Advent is a time of running, but it is a purposeful running that leads to the "rich reward of eternal life." May this blessing be ours not only during Advent, but throughout the liturgical year.

To Ponder

- Faith, hope, and charity are concretely played out in my life in these ways . . .

- Advent is a time to run the race of life and leads me to . . .

Prayer

You give us the gift of the virtues of faith, hope, and charity,
O wondrous God,
and invite us to live them
as we journey toward our eternal home with you.
Be with us as we direct our lives to your purposes
and hear your voice leading us toward fullness of Life.
We ask this through Christ our Lord. Amen.

5.2 GLORIOUS BIRTH HAS ILLUMINATED

Roman Missal Text

> May the God of infinite goodness,
> who by the Incarnation of his Son has driven darkness from
>   the world
> and by that glorious Birth has illumined this most holy night (day),
> drive far from you the darkness of vice
> d illumine your hearts with the light of virtue.
> R. Amen.
> May God, who willed that the great joy
> of his Son's saving Birth be announced to shepherds by the Angel,
> fill your minds with the gladness he gives
> and make you heralds of his Gospel.
> R. Amen.
> And may God, who by the Incarnation
> brought together the earthly and heavenly realm,
> ill you with the gift of his peace and favor
> and make you sharers with the Church in heaven.
> R. Amen.
>
> —Blessings at the End of Mass, no. 2, The Nativity of the Lord

Reflection

In the northern hemisphere, after the summer solstice, the days begin to grow shorter and the nights longer. By the time Advent comes around, darkness has lengthened beyond the hours of light. Christmas occurs at the time of the year when the darkness is longest. Into this darkness comes the Divine Son who dispels all darkness and illuminates not only the holy night of Christmas, but even more so the darkness of our hearts and minds. This glorious Birth has illuminated everything, changing dramatically even our relationship with God. This glorious Birth unites the "earthly and heavenly realm," bringing all together once again into the peace of God's reign.

This blessing associates darkness with vice and illumination with virtue. Without Christ, and following the way of the Good News that he taught us, we live in darkness, and our works are the evil that weakens or even destroys our relationships with God and each other. With Christ, and living the Gospel, we live in the glorious light of his Resurrection, and our works are the goodness that strengthens our relationships with God and each other. Christ lights our way on the journey toward fullness of Life, our lifetime of walking with him toward our final destiny with God for all eternity.

The Incarnation ushered in the Light of the world. This Light, in his very Being, joined earth and heaven as had never before been possible. Jesus is the Son of God at the same time he is the Son of Mary. He is a Divine Being, the Second Person of the Most Holy Trinity, at the same time that he is fully human, like us in everything except sin. Jesus' Incarnation closed the chasm between the holiness of heaven and the limiting mortality of earth. While living on this earth, we still will suffer and die; we still grapple with our own human weaknesses and our free choice to choose vice over virtue. At the same time, however, we already enjoy the gift of Life that Jesus' Incarnation brought to us. This Life is the very Life of God; it fills us with peace because it is a foretaste now of the destiny to which God invites the faithful follower of Jesus.

This gift of Life calls us to be "heralds of [the] Gospel," of the Good News of God's reign come upon us. We are to announce by the very way we live that we are in a season of God's peace and favor, that God's heavenly realm is stronger than all the tyrants in the earthly realm that might entice us away from God's desires for us. Jesus' Incarnation is the birth of new Life and salvation, the promise of health and well-being that is already a share in the heavenly realm. We join the shepherds and angels in singing God's praises, for the Light of God's Glory shines on us and transforms us into that same Light, a beacon to all to come to the Jesus Christ who was born our Savior and Redeemer.

To Ponder

- What illuminates my heart and brings me closer to God and others is . . .

- The Incarnation is celebrated every day when . . .

Prayer

Glorious God of the Incarnation,
you sent your Son to be born in our likeness
and in that gracious act illuminated for us the darkness of our hearts
and brought forth in us the shining Light of your Son's Presence.
Be with us as we strive to live the Gospel
and bring peace to those mired in strife,
and grant joy to those who have lost sight of your Presence and gifts.
We ask this through Christ our Lord. Amen.

5.3 SERVING GOD AND NEIGHBOR

Roman Missal Text

> May God, the Father of mercies,
> who has given you an example of love
> in the Passion of his Only Begotten Son,
> grant that, by serving God and your neighbor,
> you may lay hold of the wondrous gift of his blessing.
> R. Amen.
> So that you may receive the reward of everlasting life from him,
> through whose earthly Death
> you believe that you escape eternal death.
> R. Amen.
> And by following the example of his self-abasement,
> may you possess a share in his Resurrection.
> R. Amen.
>
> —Blessings at the End of Mass, no. 5, The Passion of the Lord

Reflection

How much is too much? If it's a matter of very hard work with little or no recompense, even a little is too much. If it's a matter of love, then no amount of giving and receiving is too much. We can never get enough of the love we have for each other. Again and again we say, "I love you" to spouse, children, parents, lasting friends, close relatives. God has pronounced the definitive "I love you" in the Only Begotten Son. Jesus has pronounced the definitive "I love you" in his willingness to accept the passion, dying on the cross so that we might share in his Life. We pronounce a definitive "I love you" when we follow "the example of his self-abasement."

Jesus' self-abasement was no false humility, no self-degradation that rendered him powerless to act. No, his self-abasement was an unprecedented self-emptying: he let go of being God so that he might become one of us. He so identified with our human nature that he suffered pain and loss, rejection and misunderstanding, and even death. He did not come among us as someone apart from us, but understood perfectly our human condition because he so perfectly lived our condition. His self-abasement raises us up beyond the dust of our own humanity to share in the wonder of his Divine Life. His humility is our exaltation.

Neither Jesus' self-abasement nor our exaltation is played out in some abstract realm. They are expressed concretely and visibly in serving God and neighbor. Serving—giving ourselves for another's good—is the way we identify with Jesus and are immersed in his Life which includes both self-abasement and exaltation. The "wondrous gift of [God's] blessing" is first and foremost the privilege of serving others as Jesus showed us so well how to do. No one is to be excluded from our serving. In Christ there is no stranger, no one undeserving of our love and attention. Self-abasement is surrendering ourselves into the hands of others so that they might live a fuller and more fulfilling life. Self-abasement is recognized in the suffering we ourselves experience when we see others not able to reach full potential, not able to become who God wants them to be. Self-abasement is an emptying of self so that others might be full of the Life that we have already been given by God.

Serving God and neighbor is an embrace of all of creation and creature in the love and care, compassion and peace in which God first created us. It is following in Jesus' footsteps of reaching out to others with a new message of dignity and worth. It is touching another with the kind of gentleness that brings wholeness and well-being. It is being the Presence of the risen Christ for others in such a way that for at least the moment of our own presence, the other is relieved of his or her alienation from all that is good. This blessing is a pledge of our own selfless determination to treat others as God has already treated us. We serve God in others.

To Ponder

- True love consists of . . .

- It is renewing and creating in that . . .

- I serve God and others in these ways . . .

Prayer

God of compassion and mercy,
send your Holy Spirit upon us to strengthen us
so that we might serve others as Jesus did.
Help us to see in others your Life and Presence
and by reaching out to them reveal to all the world
that you are all Goodness and Truth.
We ask this through Christ our Lord. Amen.

5.4   WONDROUS FLAME

Roman Missal Text

> May God, the Father of lights,
> who was pleased to enlighten the disciples' minds
> by the outpouring of the Spirit, the Paraclete,
> grant you gladness by his blessing
> and make you always abound with the gifts of the same Spirit.
> R. Amen.
> May the wondrous flame that appeared above the disciples,
> powerfully cleanse your hearts from every evil
> and pervade them with its purifying light.
> R. Amen.
> And may God, who has been pleased to unite many tongues
> in the profession of one faith,
> give you perseverance in that same faith
> and, by believing, may you journey from hope to clear vision.
> R. Amen.
>
> —Blessings at the End of Mass, no. 8, The Holy Spirit

Reflection

Fire is an image that reminds us of both destruction and creation. Escaping gas is ignited by a tiny spark and explodes in a fury of fire that destroys life and buildings all around. Fire burns down forests and prairies. Fire destroys flesh and leaves excruciatingly painful burns and unmanageable disfigurement. Fire also warms us and cooks our food. The flame of a flickering candle brings warmth and atmosphere to a special occasion and the flame of a candle or an oil lamp sends forth light when our electricity goes out. The discovery of fire by humankind is perhaps more useful and helpful than all the technological discoveries of the modern era, often hardly thought about and so taken for granted. Another fire that is easily taken for granted is the "wondrous flame that appeared above the disciples" on that first Pentecost long ago, and that settled on us when we first received the Holy Spirit at our Baptism. This flame is both destructive and creative, too.

The flame of the Holy Spirit has the power to "cleanse [our] hearts from every evil." It has the power to clear our minds of all the clutter that keeps us from turning toward God and the salvation that God offers. This flame of the Holy Spirit clears our path along the journey of life from whatever can cause us to stumble or falter in the perseverance of our faith. Unlike the flames that destroy life or buildings, this flame of the Holy Spirit destroys all that stands in the way of our being true disciples of Jesus, and so has a positive outcome.

The flame of the Holy Spirit has the power to bring about much good in and through us. It has the power to enlighten our minds so that we can clearly discern God's will for our lives. It has the power to bring us the joy of Life in the Spirit imbued with the wondrous gifts that only the Holy Spirit can give—the gifts of wisdom, understanding, counsel, reverence, knowledge, piety, and awe of the Lord (see Isaiah 11:2–3). We not only are given these gifts, but we abound in them. God assures us that we can never falter in our following Jesus, so long as we remain open to these gifts and use them as God intends.

The flame of the Holy Spirit gives us another gift, that of unity. We are united in the one Body of Christ by the indwelling of the Holy Spirit, who is in us as the risen Christ himself. It is the power of the Spirit that enables our discipleship; the power of the Spirit empowers us to be faithful and imbues us with the flame of love that makes the Gospel fruitful in our lives and in the lives of others. Our Baptism confers on us our identity as Christians, as members of the one Body of Christ. Our Baptism brings the gift of the indwelling of the Holy Spirit, and with this Divine Gift a gladness of heart that is unequaled by anything we can do or say. The wondrous flame of the Holy Spirit is with us always, even when we give in to the lures of darkness. The light of this Divine Flame can never be extinguished, for it is the very Presence of the glory of God.

To Ponder

- I experience the wondrous flame of the Holy Spirit burning brightly within me when . . . This Flame leads me to . . .

- The gift of the Holy Spirit on which I rely most is . . . It helps me to . . .

Prayer

O Triune God, Father, Son, and Holy Spirit,
you fill us with your Divine Presence and your Life and love.
Help us to surrender ourselves to your Presence
and respond with enlightened minds and gladsome hearts
to whatever you ask of us,
to wherever you lead us,
to whomever you bring into our lives.
We ask this through Christ our Lord. Amen.

5.5   MAY THE LORD'S FACE SHINE ON US

Roman Missal Text

> May the Lord bless you and keep you.
> R. Amen.
> May he let his face shine upon you
> and show you his mercy.
> R. Amen.
> May he turn his countenance towards you
> and give you his peace.
> R. Amen.
>
> —Blessings at the End of Mass, no. 9, Ordinary Time I

Reflection

We hear this blessing proclaimed as the First Reading for January 1, the Solemnity of Mary, the Holy Mother of God. Its origin is in the Old Testament Book of Numbers (6:24–26). God commands Moses to speak to Aaron and his sons—the priests of Israel—and bless them with these words. This would have been astounding at the time. In antiquity, gods were to be feared and placated. Even Israelites thought that to see the face of God meant sure death. Now, here in this blessing—the words of which are given by God—the prayer is that God's "face shine upon" the Israelites whom the priests are blessing. Such favor this blessing brings!

Face or countenance is an image used in Sacred Scripture for God's Presence. To see God's face is to see God. To have God's face shine upon others is to have God's very Being overshadow them with divine protection and help. This blessing not only shows God's favor and beneficence toward the chosen people, but also shows how beloved Israel is to God. God's love is so great for God's people that even disclosing the Divine Presence is not too much. God is turned toward Israel so long as they turn themselves toward God. God's peace is the fruit of divine-human encounter whereby there is no chasm between God's will and the people's fidelity.

January 1 is the first day of the New Year. How fitting it is to proclaim this reading/blessing from the Book of Numbers! We can ask no more of the coming year than to see God face to face, to live in God's Presence, to be favored by God's countenance turned toward us. The only really fitting New Year's resolution in the context of this blessing is to decide to live the year with our own faces turned toward God. The peace we wish for the New Year is a peace we wish for during the entire year. It is a peace borne of God's Presence and favor.

While January 1 is the day of the proclamation of the blessing as a reading, this blessing is suitable for any time during Ordinary Time—that is, it is suitable for most of the year. God's favor is not limited to one day, but is a gracious blessing poured forth upon us whenever we turn our own countenance toward God. Saying Amen to this blessing is a way of pledging ourselves to live God's will, to turn ourselves toward God in answer to all God wants of us. This blessing is a way of living in which we receive God's abundant mercy when we choose to turn our countenance away, and God's abundant blessing and Presence when we faithfully follow God's commandments and live as Jesus has taught us.

To Ponder

- I find it easiest to turn my face toward God when . . .

- I experience God's countenance shining upon me when . . .

- The blessing and peace I experience from doing God's will is . . .

Prayer

God who is ever-present to us in mercy and peace,
hear our prayer for your blessing.
May we turn our own countenance toward you in obedience and love
and receive from you all we need to be faithful all the days of our lives.
We ask this through Christ our Lord. Amen.

5.6 POUR OUT SAVING WISDOM

Roman Missal Text

> May almighty God bless you in his kindness
> and pour out saving wisdom upon you.
> R. Amen.
> May he nourish you always with the teachings of the faith
> and make you persevere in holy deeds.
> R. Amen.
> May he turn your steps towards himself
> and show you the path of charity and peace.
> R. Amen.
>
> —Blessings at the End of Mass, no. 11, Ordinary Time III

Reflection

Young Solomon, newly appointed king of Israel, was told by God in a dream to ask for anything and it would be granted. We might expect Solomon to answer that he wanted a long and peaceful reign, or great riches, or many sons. Instead, Solomon asks for something that will help him to be a good king-servant, discerning right from wrong: he asked for an understanding mind (1 Kings 3:9). Solomon became famous—even to this day—for his great wisdom. Wisdom is more than possessing vast knowledge. Wisdom is the kind of knowledge-discernment that comes from having experience. The young Solomon knew he was too young to have such experience, so he asked God for wisdom.

In this blessing, God is asked to "pour out saving wisdom upon" us. Like with Solomon, this is more than simply knowledge. We ask God to bless us with knowledge-discernment of human experience, human actions. This discernment helps us sort out the myriads of temptations and choices that come our way each day. We are bombarded with all kinds of information. God's saving wisdom helps us to filter and categorize all this information that comes our way in our daily living, so that we grow in the ability to make choices that keep us on the "path of charity and peace."

With the "teachings of the faith" we can know right from wrong and act justly. To some extent, experience teaches us this. However, until we have enough experience, we rely on the kindness of God's gift of saving wisdom and the guidance from the Church to help us discern the choices we make to keep our steps turned toward God. This wisdom cannot be a one-time blessing. Fruitful discernment of choices and actions is a lifelong task into which we continually grow. God's blessing of saving wisdom brings us to achieve the kind of well-being and wholeness that reinforces our decision-making.

When our decisions bring us peace and increase our charity toward others, we judge that they are good decisions. This is another way of stating how St. Thomas Aquinas wrote about conscience. For this angelic saint, conscience was not a little voice inside us, but rather the cumulative effect of the practical judgments we make about our lives. The formation of a good conscience is a matter of making wise and prudent decisions about the actions we undertake. If we make bad or harmful decisions, our conscience is formed badly. Therefore, our everyday experiences contribute immensely to how we live the Gospel and respond to God's call to live wisely and justly. Like Solomon of long ago, we are wise to ask God to bless us with an increase of saving wisdom. This gift assures that we are turned toward God and serve God in all we do. It assures us that we, with God's help, can "persevere in holy deeds."

To Ponder

- I am aware of God's gift of wisdom to me when . . .
  This affects decisions I make in that . . .

- The holy deeds in which I persevere are . . .

Prayer

Kind and merciful God,
you bless us with the wisdom to discern
how to live the Gospel fruitfully.
May we always receive this blessing with an open heart
and more surely turn ourselves toward you,
living the Gospel in such a way
that we witness to your reign of peace and holiness.
We ask this through Christ our Lord. Amen.

5.7   ALL CONSOLATION

Roman Missal Text

> May the God of all consolation order your days in his peace
> and grant you the gifts of his blessing.
> R. Amen.
> May he free you always from every distress
> and confirm your hearts in his love.
> R. Amen.
> So that on this life's journey
> you may be effective in good works,
> rich in the gifts of hope, faith and charity,
> and may come happily to eternal life.
> R. Amen.

—Blessings at the End of Mass, no. 12, Ordinary Time IV

Reflection

When a little child is sick, he or she naturally goes to mom or dad for comfort. The little one might crawl into the parent's lap and cuddle up for warmth and caressing. The parent knows that this will not make the child physically better; only time, medication, and proper nourishment will accomplish that. But the parent also knows that the comfort, security, and reassurance that comes from holding the child tightly and protectively is as important as the physical ministrations. Whenever we human beings suffer, we desire consolation. One of Sigmund Freud's mechanisms for coping is "misery loves company." We need the companionship, understanding, and presence of another when we are hurting.

None of us gets through life with no mishaps. Physical illnesses, emotional challenges, undue distress come crashing upon us. The more serious the mishap, the more dire the need for consolation. We might beg God to "free us always from every distress," but we all know that this will not happen. As humans, we are not in control of much of the heartache and physical ailments that come our way. When it comes to life's biggest challenges, only God can provide us with the support and divine care needed to get through whatever is causing our suffering. God is the source of all consolation.

Over and over again God has shown divine care for us humans. From creating us in the Divine Image to leading us from bondage to freedom, to giving us a Savior to show us the way to salvation, God has cared for us. God's care is marked by an amazing, divine fidelity to the divine promise to be loved and be chosen to be God's very own people. Not only God's people, but also we are, through

Baptism, made heirs of the fullness of Life as we live out our identity as the Body of Christ. Whatever distress might come our way, God is always there to hold us closely and protect us from taking a wrong path on this life's journey. We are made "rich in the gifts" God offers us so that we might not be overcome by distress, but live through it to the peace and happiness that God gives.

Because God is the source of all consolation, we are never alone in whatever life's challenges we face. Even when our family members or brothers and sisters in Christ are not present to us to help us through difficulties, God is always there, reaching out a consoling Presence to comfort and heal us. Loss and disappointment, suffering and distress are part of the human condition. How consoling to know that Jesus himself shared in this human condition, knows firsthand our distress, and is the perfect intercessor before the Father, so that we receive all consolation and live in God's peace.

To Ponder

- The distress and difficulties with which I presently deal are . . .
- I am aware of God's consolation and Presence when . . .
- I am at peace with God, myself, and others when . . .

Prayer

God of all consolation,
you never forsake us, but always are present to us in our times of need.
Strengthen us to face with courage whatever distress comes our way
and help us never to lose sight of your care and love.
Be with us as we grow in our ability to see the needs of others
and reach out to them with the care and love you show us,
recognizing that you extend your care to them through us.
We ask this through Christ our Lord. Amen.

5.8   MARY'S PROTECTION

Roman Missal Text

> May God, who through the childbearing of the Blessed
>   Virgin Mary
> willed in his great kindness to redeem the human race,
> be pleased to enrich you with his blessing.
> R. Amen.
> May you know always and everywhere the protection of her,
> through whom you have been found worthy to receive the author
>   of life.
> R. Amen.
> May you, who have devoutly gathered on this day,
> carry away with you the gifts of spiritual joys
>   and heavenly rewards.
> R. Amen.
>
> —Blessings at the End of Mass, no. 15, The Blessed Virgin Mary

Reflection

In so many ways Mary was a young maiden with the same hopes and aspirations as other girls of her time. As a little girl, she probably dreamed of finding a strong, good husband and bearing many children to make them happy in their old age. Little could Mary have imagined, however, the utter goodness of her spouse, Joseph, the wonder of her Son, Jesus, and the challenges that her motherhood would bring. What mother wishes to stand at the site of her son's execution? What mother wishes to hear her son being ridiculed and rejected? What mother wishes to have her heart pierced with sorrow (see Luke 2:35)? Through it all, Mary is the ever faithful Mother, always responding with a "Here am I, the servant of the Lord; let it be with me according to your word" (Luke 1:38).

Mary not only bore the child Jesus, she also bears each of us who are sisters and brothers in the Body of Christ. The same fidelity and loving service that Mary showered on her Divine Son she gives to us, her children. Mary is God's blessing for us, a mother who shows us what fidelity to God's will is, who shows us devotion to her Son, who shows us an unfailing protection as only a mother can show. Mary's relationship with her Son spills over in a relationship with each of us. The care she showed to her Son is the same care she shows us each day of our lives. To be blessed "always and everywhere" with the protection of Mary is to be assured that, through her help, we can be faithful to the way of life that Jesus came to teach us.

The sorrows Mary faced in her life did not sway her from her utter fidelity to God's will. She is the model to whom we look when our own daily burdens seem too much. Rather than go our own way, we are privileged to have a heavenly Mother who understands our needs and never forsakes interceding before God on our behalf. Mary is the great kindness of God given us so that we might be enriched in every blessing and come to the salvation that her Divine Son came to gain for us.

Mary was faithful in all God asked of her; for that she enjoys the fullness of Life as she stands in God's Presence giving God praise forever. The "gifts of spiritual joys and heavenly rewards," which she now has, will be ours if we are faithful to discerning and doing God's will as she was. Like Mary, we are servants of the Lord ready and willing at all times to do as God wills. Like Mary, we bear for others the Divine Son when we reach out to those in need with a healing and consoling hand. Like Mary, we look with wonder and awe upon this Divine Son, who came to lift us out of the darkness of sin and selfishness and lead us to that marvelous light that promises fullness of Life.

To Ponder

- I most often turn to Mary when . . .

- Like Mary, I bear Christ for others when I . . .

Prayer

Almighty God,
you sent your Only-Begotten Son to be born of the Virgin Mary
and to share our human condition in all things except sin.
Bless us with a deeper appreciation and love for Mary, our Mother,
and help us to be the faithful servant
committed to doing your will in all things.
We ask this through Christ our Lord. Amen.

5.9 JOYS OF THE HOMELAND

Roman Missal Text

May God, the glory and joy of the Saints,
who has caused you to be strengthened
by means of their outstanding prayers,
bless you with unending blessings.
R. Amen.
Freed through their intercession from present ills
and formed by the example of their holy way of life,
may you be ever devoted
to serving God and your neighbor.
R. Amen.
So that, together with all,
you may possess the joys of the homeland,
where Holy Church rejoices
that her children are admitted in perpetual peace
to the company of the citizens of heaven.
R. Amen.

—Blessings at the End of Mass, no. 18, All Saints

Reflection

The Book of Revelation, the last book of the New Testament, paints a beautiful picture of the heavenly liturgy where all the angels and saints are forever before God's throne singing "Hosanna" and "Alleluia" and "Amen." These are the "citizens of heaven" whom one day we hope to join in offering God unending praise and thanksgiving: "To the one seated on the throne and to the Lamb be blessing and honor and glory and might forever and ever!" (Revelation 5:13).

For all of us, a home is more than bricks and mortar and a place to hang our hat. There can be no home without people and not just people together, but people united in a common bond of relationship (not necessarily blood relationship) and purpose. We who are baptized in Christ try to make our earthly homes places where God is at the center. Our reason for being is to lead a "holy way of life." In these homes, present ills are assuaged by the support and strength given to each other. The common purpose of those who live in these homes is serving God and neighbor to the best of their ability.

Our earthly homes, nevertheless, are temporary. We are not destined for this life, but for the next. Our ultimate home is to be with God and all the angels and saints in that heavenly dwelling, which is truly our homeland, our destiny, where

God from the very beginning of time has called us to be. There is no great chasm between our earthly and heavenly homes; instead, they are separated by the death that Jesus has conquered. The link between our two homes is the outstanding prayers of intercession the saints constantly make on our behalf before the Presence of God. Another link is that the saints form us by their example to live God's will through serving God and neighbor. They show us by their lives which we remember throughout the liturgical year that it is very possible to be faithful to living the Gospel. Their lives are proof of fidelity and the encouragement we need to face whatever present ills come our way.

We will "possess the joys of the homeland" one day; that is God's promise and the assurance the saints give us. That homeland will be free from all ills, will be marked by perpetual peace, and will unite us to the company of the citizens of heaven. On that day we will share fully in the bond of being members of the Body of Christ, we will rejoice in each other's goodness, and praise and thank God forever for counting us among the Saints who unceasingly stand in God's marvelous Presence.

To Ponder

- The saint upon whom I depend most for strength is . . .

- The life I've been shown through this saint is . . .

- My earthly home looks like . . . My heavenly home looks like . . .

Prayer

God of glory and unending joy,
the angels and saints in heaven are constantly in your Presence
    bowing down in adoration before you.
Through their intercession
may we be strengthened to live a holy way of life
and one day join them as citizens in heaven living with you forever.
We ask this through Christ our Lord. Amen.

5.10   THE HOPE OF RISING AGAIN

Roman Missal Text

May the God of all consolation bless you,
for in his unfathomable goodness he created the human race
and in the Resurrection of his Only Begotten Son
he has given believers the hope of rising again.
R. Amen.
To us who are alive, may God grant pardon for our sins
and to all the dead, a place of light and peace.
R. Amen.
So may we all live happily for ever with Christ,
whom we believe truly rose from the dead.
R. Amen.

—Blessings at the End of Mass, no. 20, In Celebrations for the Dead

Reflection

Can we imagine, when someone we love dies, getting through the sense of loss and great sadness without the help of our faith? If we didn't have a strong belief in eternal Life, how could we accept a total finality of human death? Our belief in Jesus and the Good News of salvation that he brings gives us strength and hope during these difficult times. Without this hope, our sense of loss would sever all relationship with our loved one. Jesus came to offer to us consolation and the "hope of rising again." Our hope is built on the firm foundation of Jesus himself, who accepted death in obedience to his Father's will. For that obedience, he was raised up to new Life.

Risen Life is different from being raised from the dead, as some stories in the Gospels depict. Jesus raised the widow of Nain's son from the dead (see Luke 7:14–15), Jairus' daughter (see Luke 8:53–55), and Lazarus (see John 11:43–44). In all these cases (and, no doubt, others that the Gospels do not record) Jesus returned the dead people to the same life that they had known. So this being raised from the dead is different from Jesus' Resurrection; Jesus' risen Life is forever. When we die, we follow Jesus into the risen Life and glory that is his. We, too, will live forever. We will perpetually be in "a place of light and peace," spending all eternity contemplating the beauty of God's Presence.

This blessing reminds us, in addition to our having the "hope of rising again," that we must also seek pardon for our sins. God is a compassionate God who forgives everything we have ever done that harms our relationships with the Divine One and each other. All we need do is express our sorrow and turn our lives back to God. The Church places great value on the Sacrament of Penance, for in this visible sign of God's mercy and forgiveness we are assured of increasing or restoring God's Life within us. This sacrament is not a negative rattling off a list of our wrongdoing, but is a positive admission of our need for God, our own weakness, and our desire to live as God wishes us to live.

If we are assured of forgiveness—and we are—then what is purgatory and why do we continue to pray for our beloved dead? Purgatory is not about forgiveness—God has showered that upon us in God's infinite mercy and compassion. Purgatory is a cleansing of ourselves of the effects of turning from God. Any sin is harmful to our relationship with God and each other. It weakens—or in the case of mortal sin, completely severs—our relationship with God. As soon as we express sorrow, our sin is forgiven. But we still have the work of building the relationships and growing in our love for God and each other. Purgatory is how the Church describes the time we spend after death purifying our relationships and growing into the Presence of God. Our prayers for our beloved dead strengthen and encourage them in this purifying process.

Because Jesus has gone before us in death and Resurrection, we who believe ought to have no fear of our human death. In fact, we ought to look forward to it, pray for a happy death, and anticipate the fullness of Life that death opens for us. We who believe in the "hope of rising again" can stand tall in face of any adversity for we know that the best is yet to come. Our confidence is in God; our hope lies in the risen Christ.

To Ponder

- I experience a place of light and peace and know my loved ones have a share in it when . . .

- When I pray for my beloved dead, I believe that . . .

- For me, everlasting life is . . .

Prayer

God of hope and peace,
you raised your Son to new Life
and in that Resurrection assure us of a share in that same Life of glory.
Help us to seek pardon for our sins
and always to be prepared for that moment when death comes
as we enter into everlasting Life and joy with you.
We ask this through Christ our Lord. Amen.

5.11 STAND FIRM UNDER GOD'S PROTECTION

Roman Missal Text

> Be propitious to your people, O God,
> that, freed from every evil,
> they may serve you with all their heart
> and ever stand firm under your protection.
> Through Christ our Lord.
>
> —Prayers over the People, no. 8

Reflection

God is *propitious*—so wonderfully favorable toward us. God is tender with us from the act of creation itself to watching over us to the point that not a hair on our head will be disturbed (see Luke 21:18; also, Luke 12:22–32). We pray that God be propitious to us, but it is almost a pointless prayer. God is always abundantly good to us. Only we can reject the goodness God offers; only we can reject God's favor; only we can reject how much God desires to care for us. Our prayer to be "freed from every evil" is an important one, for when we give in to evil we estrange ourselves from God and God's care.

God not only cares for us, God also protects us from whatever might harm us. This is surely a comforting thought. This doesn't mean that nothing harmful will ever beset us. We will still deal with sickness and death, temptation and self-centeredness. That is the human condition; that is our heritage as part of the human family. However, we also belong to God through our Baptism; we are also members of the Body of Christ, heirs of God. We "stand firm under [God's] protection" when we turn ourselves unselfishly toward God and surrender ourselves to doing faithfully whatever God asks of us. Even when bad things seem to come our way, God is still there protecting us, because the only bad thing we need stalwartly to avoid is alienation from God. Nothing else really matters so long as we are in right relationship with God, so long as we maintain the friendship with God that opens us to receive divine protection.

Divine protection is also the source of our commitment to and energy for serving God with all our hearts. We serve God by serving others. The more we reach out of ourselves toward others, the more closely we connect ourselves to the Divine Presence and the protection that brings. God's protection is a canopy of love over us, a mantle of the Holy Spirit who makes all things possible through us. Confident that we do not act alone, but with God's help, we can make known the Good News of God's offer of salvation through Christ Jesus. God's protection keeps us on the path toward the fullness of Life for which we were created. God's protection eases the effects of original sin and enables us to make the right choices that mean fruitful serving with all our hearts. So long as we "stand firm under [God's] protection," we are assured of receiving into our very being God's care, God's Presence, God's help in all we do.

To Ponder

- God's protection means to me . . . I am most able to stand firm under God's protection when . . .

- My serving others is serving God in these ways . . .

Prayer

O God,
you favor us with all good things
and protect us with holy jealousy for your service.
Help us to risk serving others in generous ways
so that we might grow in our love for you.
May we be faithful to the Good News Jesus taught
and so one day enjoy the fullness of Life with you for all eternity.
We ask this through Christ our Lord. Amen.

5.12 SHOW DEDICATION TO GOD'S NAME

Roman Missal Text

> Keep your family, we pray, O Lord,
> in your constant care,
> so that, under your protection,
> they may be free from all troubles
> and by good works show dedication to your name.
> Through Christ our Lord.
>
> —Prayers over the People, no. 11

Reflection

In biblical times, one's name said something about who the person is or was to do in life. Key Scriptural passages revealing the history of God's saving deeds include name changes indicating a change in life, a greater dedication and obedience to God's ways. For example, Abram's name was changed to Abraham, and he became the father of many nations (see Genesis 17:5); Jacob became Israel, the father of Joseph and his brothers (see Genesis 32:28); Simon became Peter, the rock upon which Jesus' Church is built (see Luke 6:14 and Matthew 16:18); Saul became Paul, the great apostle to the Gentiles (Acts 13:9). When Gabriel appears to Zechariah and Mary to announce that they would each have a son, they are told the name they were to give them: John and Jesus. When Jesus appears to Mary Magdalene after the Resurrection, he only needs to say her name and she recognizes him (see John 20:16).

Perhaps the most important Scripture event pertaining to name happens in the exchange between God and Moses at the burning bush. God calls Moses to go to Pharaoh in Egypt so Moses can bring the Israelites out of Egypt, from slavery to the land flowing with milk and honey that God would give them (see Genesis 3:1–15). Moses is aware of his relationship with the Pharaoh, and knows he needs a greater authority than his own in order for his request for the Israelites' freedom to be secured. The authority he seeks can be nothing less than God's own, so Moses asks God for the name of who sent him to reveal to Pharaoh. To know God's name is to know who God is.

We strive all our lives to pronounce God's holy name and come to know who God is. The second of the Ten Commandments requires that we "shall not make wrongful use of the name of the Lord your God" (Exodus 20:7; Deuteronomy 5:11). To speak God's holy name without the proper reverence is to speak to and of God without reverence. It is to defame God's very Being. God's name makes present God to us, and in face of this Divine Presence, we can only speak with awe and praise. To pronounce God's holy name is to recognize God as our Sovereign who created us, sustains us by constant care, and keeps us under divine protection.

We must do more than speak God's holy name, although that is precisely what we do in prayer. To keep God's name on our lips all day is to keep God ever before us as the center of our lives. However, God asks more of us. When we do good works, we reverence God's name. Our good works make visible to those around us that God cares and protects. Our good works in themselves can be fruitful prayer raised to God, praising God for the gifts given us to act toward others as Jesus taught us. Our good works "show dedication to [God's] name" in that we are manifesting the very goodness of God. When we do good, we act like God, we live out of our own being the very Being of God who dwells within us and acts through us. As we grow in awareness of this great privilege of bringing the goodness of God to others, we grow in our love and appreciation for God's constant Presence to us. Our "dedication to [God's] name" shows that we accept God as our all.

To Ponder

- The good works I do that bring others God's goodness and Presence is . . .

- I reverence God's name in prayer when I say . . .

- I reverence God's name in my good works when I . . .

Prayer

Holy God,
your name is above every name,
your Presence is visible goodness,
your protection keeps us in your constant care.
May we utter your name in prayer often during our days,
and do good works that bring reverence to your name.
May our dedication as your servants
bring honor and glory to your holy name.
We ask this through Christ our Lord. Amen.

5.13 Doing Something Truly Worthy

Roman Missal Text

> Look with favor on your family, O Lord,
> and bestow your endless mercy on those who seek it:
> and just as without your mercy,
> they can do nothing truly worthy of you,
> so through it,
> may they merit to obey your saving commands.
> Through Christ our Lord.
>
> —Prayers over the People, no. 16

Reflection

Self-worth is important for anyone to grow into a healthy and whole human being. When God gave us the second great commandment, to love others as ourselves (see Leviticus 19:18), the issue was not that we love ourselves in terms of self-centeredness or narcissistic egotism. Without due regard for ourselves, we cannot reach out of ourselves toward another. This reaching out is a selfless love that imitates God's love. This selfless love bestows on us the greatest self-worth because this love aligns us with God and how God acts toward us. Healthy self-worth is the source of our ability to be generous and kind, merciful and forgiving, loving and caring. It is a recognition not of what we make of ourselves, but of what God has made and is making of us.

This blessing prayer asks God to look with favor on us so that, with God's endless mercy we can do something truly worthy of God. Without God's mercy, we can do "nothing truly worthy" of God. How can we, mere creatures, do anything truly worthy of God? The answer to this all-important question lies in this blessing prayer. We do something worthy of God when we "obey [God's] saving commands."

Obeying God is more than minimally keeping the Ten Commandments, the Beatitudes, and the works of mercy. God's saving commands surely include these, but go well beyond them to the values that lie beneath the commandments themselves. Moreover, all of these values are concrete ways of showing that we love God, self, and the other. For example, the First Commandment tells us to have no other gods before our God of the covenant. No, we may not be guilty of the idolatry the Israelites fell into even before Moses could come down from Mount Sinai with the Ten Commandments (see Exodus 32:8 and Deuteronomy 9:12). But we have our own idols: keeping up with the Joneses and our own selfish desires, to name but two. The underlying value of this commandment is to keep God at the center of our lives and live out of that Divine Presence. Other values underlying God's commandments include giving ourselves sufficient rest to be healthy, eating right, respecting property and the environment, respecting the person of another, being truthful, caring for the poor, being willing to face persecution for the sake of the Gospel. These and many other values map out for us a way of living that is in obedience to God's saving commands.

Living these values is no easy life; it is much easier to seek our own values and wants. But this latter course of action never leads to doing what is "truly worthy of" God. Living God's values always is "truly worthy of" God because these values come from the very God whom we choose to serve. We receive God's favor when we surrender ourselves to the life to which God calls us, a life flowing from Gospel values, and the very life of Jesus. Living this way assures us of God's mercy. We cannot make a better choice for our own salvation.

To Ponder

- Actions that I have done lately that have been "truly worthy of" God are . . .

- God's commandment that I find easiest to keep is . . . the most difficult . . . The values that underlie these commandments are . . .

Prayer

God of covenant and commandment,
your mercy guides us in all things
and your strength helps us to be worthy of your saving deeds.
Draw us to your Divine Son and the life he taught us;
help us live Gospel values in such a way
as to bring you praise for your great care for us.
Strengthen us when we falter and stray
from the path of your commands.
We ask this through Christ our Lord. Amen.

5.14 GROWTH THROUGH TEACHINGS

Roman Missal Text

> Keep your family safe, O Lord, we pray,
> and grant them the abundance of your mercies,
> that they may find growth
> through the teachings and the gifts of heaven.
> Through Christ our Lord.
>
> —Prayers over the People, no. 25

Reflection

We constantly ask God for an abundance of mercies, although God grants us all mercy because God desires to be in relationship with us, overcoming any alienation we might have from God. God seeks us and extends to us all mercy so that no matter how often or how far we stray from the path of truth and righteousness, God is always there beckoning us back to divine care. Our safety lies not in our own efforts, but in God's great care. Our human lives are characterized by stumbling and bumbling. God lifts us out of our chaos and blesses us with "teachings and the gifts of heaven" so that we might come back to the sure path of salvation.

Teachers are greatly underrated in our society. The best ones know well that teaching is not a nine to five job, but a lifelong vocation of ministry to those who seek to grow in knowledge. The best ones also know well that teaching is more than dumping information and facts into pliable minds. Teaching is forming both the mind and heart, forming the whole self into a mature and self-reliant individual who can successfully embrace the tasks of adulthood. Good teaching includes imparting values; teachers teach with their own lives and example far more than with books and rulers. Parents are the first and most important teachers. "Do as I say and not as I do" never works. Children have an uncanny way of seeing through dishonesty and insincerity. They want good role models in parents and teachers and other adults, because actions truly do speak louder than words.

The greatest teacher who ever lived was the Word of God spoken so eloquently that the Second Person of the Trinity became incarnate. Jesus spent his public life teaching us how to live, how to love, how to care for one another. He taught not only with words, though; he taught by his own actions. He taught us to live by living his own life in absolute and unwavering conformity to God's will. He taught us to love by reaching out even to his enemies with forgiveness. He taught us how to care by healing and helping others. When we read the Gospels— those records of Jesus' life and teaching, his good actions and unselfish surrender—we learn of how Jesus taught by the way he lived. He taught us through his ministry. He taught us by accepting suffering and death on our behalf. He taught us after the Resurrection by not abandoning us, but promising to send the Holy Spirit, that great teacher of wisdom and counsel.

The gifts of heaven that we receive when we heed Jesus' teaching are freely given us so that we might live as Jesus did. We are given the Gift of the Holy Spirit, the gift of God's Presence, the gift of witnessing faithfully to God's goodness and love for us, the gift of being followers of Jesus, the gift of salvation. These gifts are not taught, but they are given us so that the teachings of Jesus might become more real in our lives. They help us discern what Jesus meant in his preaching and parables, in his prayers for us, in his acts of nourishment that help us grow into the beloved children of God and heirs of heaven that he desires us to be. Jesus' teaching is the sure path to everlasting happiness. May we learn well and grow readily!

To Ponder

- What Jesus' life most importantly teaches me is . . .
- What my life teaches others is . . .
- Jesus' teaching has helped me grow in these ways . . .

Prayer

God of wisdom and counsel,
you sent the Divine Word in the flesh
to teach and witness to us the path to salvation.
Help us to be open to all Christ opens up to us in the Scriptures,
in our daily prayers,
and in the liturgies which we celebrate with such joy.
We ask this through that same Christ our Lord. Amen.

5.15 Go . . .

Roman Missal Text

> Go forth, the Mass is ended.
> Or
> Go and announce the Gospel of the Lord.
> Or
> Go in peace, glorifying the Lord by your life.
> Or
> Go in peace.
> Thanks be to God.
>
> —The Concluding Rites, no. 144

Final Thoughts

Before Jesus ascended into heaven, he gave a simple but far-reaching command to us: he commissioned us to go and make disciples and baptize in the name of the Trinity (see Matthew 28:16–20). *Go. . . .* This is the command. We are not to sit on our haunches and simply enjoy the good gifts God has given us, keeping them for ourselves. No, we are to go out to the ends of the earth—and we are so blessed at the end of Mass to do this—and share those gifts with others, make God's name known, spread the Good News Jesus came to reveal to us.

At liturgy, we make present the Mystery of Christ. Time collapses so that those events of long ago are not simply past events over and done with, but are events taking place sacramentally here and now, shaping us into being ever more prefect members of the Body of Christ. It is all too easy for us to miss the great import of liturgy. Our celebrations are not simply an hour to get through, nor are they simply social times for us to gather as a community, nor are they private prayer times. Our liturgical celebrations bring together the diverse members of the Body of Christ, beg of us a surrender to God's Presence and action in Word and Sacrament, and transform us into being the Church made visible. We don't simply *go* to liturgy; we gather for liturgy, where our identity is deepened and our commitment to the Gospel is strengthened.

One of the great concerns about liturgy of Pope Benedict XVI was that liturgy not stay within the brick-and-mortar walls where we celebrate. He was anxious that we understand that celebrating liturgy is a way of celebrating Christian living. At liturgy, we celebrate the Mystery of Christ; he is the focus; he reveals to us the Father and Spirit. When the third edition of *The Roman Missal* was newly translated and implemented in the United State on the First Sunday of Advent, 2011, something new besides a translation was there. We now have four dismissals, two of which Pope Benedict himself chose to be included in this Missal. Each says something a bit different about how we are to *go*.

The key word in the first Dismissal, "Go forth, the Mass is ended," is "forth." It is true that the Mass has ended. Mass is the ritual expression of the Eucharist, but it is not the complete expression. We ourselves have been nourished on Word and Sacrament, transformed into the very Body of Christ, which we eat and drink. The ritual celebration ends; it unfolds in time and space. But that is not all there is to Eucharist. We are to go forth to be Eucharist for all those we meet. We are to go forth to bring the Presence of the Body of Christ to others.

The key word in the second choice for the Dismissal (added by Pope Benedict), "Go and announce the Gospel of the Lord," is "announce." We are sent forth from Mass to live what we have celebrated. We announce our Christian life and Creed not by words, but by the way we live the Gospel. This is why the proclamation of the Gospel is absolutely central to the Liturgy of the Word. During this time, we hear proclaimed and preached the life that Jesus lived. We learn what it means to be a follower of Christ. We learn how we ought to live. At the conclusion of the Mass, we go forth, eager to live the Gospel and announce it faithfully by our own faithful way of living.

The key word in the third choice for the Dismissal (also added by Pope Benedict), "Go in peace, glorifying the Lord by your life," is "glorify." This dismissal begins with the same three words as does the fourth and final choice for Dismissal, but embellishes it with the Holy Father's concern about living the liturgy. We do not simply go back to our everyday living after Mass as before, because now we are different. We have encountered God during our Eucharistic celebration. We have surrendered to God's desires for us, and now when we go forth, we do so fortified with God's grace and blessing. The way we live—as Jesus lived—glorifies God in the same way that Jesus' whole life glorified the Father (see John 17:1–5). God asks nothing more of us than living as Jesus did. The peace with which we leave Mass is the same peace that Jesus bestowed upon the disciples when he appeared to them after the Resurrection (see John 20:21, 26; Luke 24:36). At Eucharist, we encounter and receive the risen Christ; we become that risen Presence for others. When we are faithful to our going forth from Mass to live who we are, the peace we experience is the gift of Life rendered to those who never cease glorifying God by their lives.

We answer the Dismissal with "Thanks be to God." Our gratitude is not about leaving the space of worship, but about the privilege of living the relationship to which God has called us. We are one in the Body of Christ. We are now to be the Presence of Christ, going forth to all the ends of the earth to announce the Good News of God's tender care and unequaled love.

To Ponder

• When I am blessed and dismissed from Mass, . . .

• I find it easiest to connect what I celebrate at Mass with how I am to live my life when . . .

Prayer

Gracious God,
you entrust to us the mission of your Divine Son
    when we are sent forth from Mass
to live what we have celebrated.
Be with us as we strive to be faithful
    to this exalted calling,
as we grow in our ability to announce the Gospel
    by the way we live.
Make our everyday prayer be fruitful
so that we come to Mass prepared to encounter you
    in all your Divine Majesty
and be transformed into ever more perfect members
    of the Body of Christ.
May we always and everywhere glorify you with all our being.
We ask this through Christ our Lord. Amen.

Our response, "Thanks be to God," our gratitude must spill over in a hunger to pray more deeply the Eucharistic liturgy, to savor its beauty and richness, to let its imagery and prayer seep deep into our very being. We never finish praying the Eucharist. We never finish delving into its meaning. We never finish plumbing its gifts to us. We never finish . . .

Go in peace, glorifying the Lord by your life.